With
Lori Bell

The Yes Process
Discover the Journey of
Becoming Yourself

Lori R. Bell

Lori R. Bell

ISBN: 1534938346
ISBN-13: 978-1534938342

To order bulk copies of this book, contact the author at support@theyesprocess.com or 803-250-LIFE (5433)

DEDICATION

*For every spiritual seeker who dares to follow the path of truth,
no matter where it leads.*

PRAISE FOR
THE YES PROCESS

"Lori is a Divine "wake-up call" in human form; and The Yes Process is The Dawn. What I've been able to process, produce, and perforate in my own transformation has been nothing short of life changing. Although the unveiling of my journey is still underway, I take with me the cured satisfaction in knowing the voyage is not something I need to fear, and everything I already am." **Taylor, Desoto, TX**

"If you're looking for the real deal, look no further than Lori Bell. This woman knows the power of example, and her example has helped me become more mindful in my life, more focused on the things that really matter, and those in turn have helped me truly find happiness. Lori doesn't just make you feel like you can do anything, she makes you believe it." **Mary Lent, Military Spouse/ Veteran**

"The work you're doing is so important. You have a way of inspiring people that is truly powerful — I saw it the moment I met you way back in the spring of 2011. The Yes Process message gets my attention, and helps me tap into the energy I need to move me forward. It reminds me that the only person who can truly move my life forward is me." **Melissa Rayworth, Writer/Blogger**

"I just wanted to let you know how awesome I think The Yes Process has been for me! I've been struggling with losing weight because of stress with my husband's deployment as well as not having that support system physically there. I've tried different strategies for weight loss, but The Yes Process actually helps me change my whole state of being for good and not just losing weight! Once I saw your article in Military Spouse Magazine I jumped straight to my computer to start the process. It's already helped tremendously!! I want to thank you so much for all you do to help so many people to achieve their dreams to be the person they want to BE. You're AWESOME!" –**Brittanni, Military Spouse**

On Using Prophetic and Intuitive Gifts:

"I am 18 years old. Lori interpreted a dream for me that helped me see how I was really letting go happiness from my life. She helped me to work on myself too. I must say her interpretation was quite accurate and I liked her work a lot." **Roma, Pakistan**

"I enjoyed having Lori interpret my dream. Her interpretation was very detailed and straight to the point. I thought it was just a silly dream. But after getting it interpreted I realized it revealed the feelings I had stuffed down. As I am at a time in life where I'm doing my inner work, it showed me I still have unresolved things I have to work on." **Layette Lanette, Trenton NJ**

"I had a dream a few weeks ago that was weighing on my heart and mind pretty heavily. I knew that it was metaphorical and trying to tell me something, but I couldn't figure out what. I consulted Lori and she gave me an interpretation of the dream that really resonated with me and made me look at my life from a different perspective. Now I feel like I understand what the dream was trying to tell me and how to take action on it. Lori did a great job breaking it down in concrete terms. Now it's up to me to change some patterns in my life for the better, based on the interpretation. Thanks Lori!" **Georgia Schrubbe, Charleston SC, www.georgiaschrubbe.com**

Social Media Love

"You ma'am…please know that there is at least one that

NEEDED this, and it was me! Thank you, THANK YOU, THANK YOU for your transparency and your obedience. Sharing IS caring and I APPRECIATE you very much!" **Danyel Walker**

"I needed this. I was under the illusion that I am alone in the natural and it blocked my view to see the spiritual. I am accepting my divine help and at first I was resisting because I didn't know what was happening. But it's all so clear to me now. Thank you, Lori, for putting this out there for people like me to understand what is happening on our path!" **Lizzy, Cape Town, South Africa**

"Thank you Ms. Lori! It is extremely hard when you walk away from religion, mainly because there is no spiritual place of worship for truth seekers, or none that I'm aware of. You feel completely lost. Thank you for always maintaining your integrity, despite any negative comments thrown at you. I admire your courage." **Aba Mensima, Michigan, USA**

"Thank you for all the encouragement. You have no idea how big the impact is in what I am going through. Continue being the light for many others." **Tabogo Kekaha, South Africa Pretoria Atteridgeville**

CONTENTS

PREFACE

There will come a moment in your life when you reach the end of yourself. When all of your striving will end, and you get to the place when you know that all is well with you. There will come a moment when the fire of determination to learn the truth about who you really are will be ignited, and you are no longer willing to settle for what you've been handed.

That moment is now.

Welcome to The Yes Process.

The Yes Process is not a single event in your life, although that is where it starts. Usually something will get your attention and shake you awake, so to speak. It is not about forcefully taking back the reigns of a life in disarray. It is not about bringing your weapons of order and discipline to the fight. You will feel at times that "fighting" is how you should win back your liberty. But fighting is completely counter to the work you are about to face.

The Yes Process is a lifestyle of committed yes's, where the only guarantee you have is what your faith has shown you. The only assurance is that your own heart work of self-forgiveness, self-love, self-acceptance and gratitude will carve out a path for you that will leave you overflowing with the fullness of your own being. It is a lifestyle of sweet surprises, a heart-first-head-second way of being, where you naturally thrive in the beauty of your own magic.

I have to warn you though. It's simple. But it ain't easy. And that's why I wrote this book for you.

My journey into The Yes Process began in 2007 after I separated from the U.S. Air Force, although I had no name for it then. I had built a nice comfortable cushion around my heart and my work for ten years in the Air Force. I was safe there. Everything was predictable in terms of who I was, where I was, and what I was there to do. I knew my mission, who I was working for and what I was working with. When I left it, it felt like moving backwards. I was no longer an officer managing millions of dollars of budget and leading a staff of people. I was now Mrs. Officer to my active duty husband and Mom to my three children. Talk about a blow to my ambitious ego.

So even though saying goodbye to all that ego-boosting prestige was liberating, it was also scary and a little sad. My boundaries were gone. I was now free to explore whatever I wanted. But what does that look like? Where's the roadmap? Where do I even start?

I didn't have the answers so I worked hard at creating projects and doing anything that looked like the fast track to success. As a military spouse I reached the professional pinnacle, being named *Military Spouse Magazine* and *Armed Forces Insurance 2010 Military Spouse of the Year*. With that award came the media blitz. I was interviewed live on *CNN*, my mom and I were interviewed live on *Fox & Friends*, I was named one of Lifetime Television's *Remarkable Women* of 2010, and I made a live appearance on *Good Morning America*. That year, Norah Roberts visited our home for an exclusive segment on *NBC Nightly News with Brian Williams* for their *Making A Difference* story.

And then in 2012 an amazing opportunity dropped in my lap. I was hand-picked to be one of 30 military spouses to spend a private day with Oprah for a *Oprah's Favorite Things* taping exclusively for military spouses. We were showered with gifts, recognition and more opportunities as we were self-named and self-appointed "Oprah's MilSpouses."

In 2013, my husband and I were invited to attend a private celebrity brunch event hosted by Eva Longoria and *Newsweek*. The room was packed, and there we were, knocking elbows with Hollywood film producer Harvy Weinstein and actress Kerry Washington, General (ret) Colin Powell and Madeline Albright. It was where Hollywood stars met political and governmental leaders…and ordinary people like me.

I thought I had made it. Life was grand! I was finally being *seen* and recognized, loved and adored. Me, lil' country girl from Swansea, SC was in the same breathing space as superstars!

Only, that wasn't it. I had done all that stuff and looked in the mirror and still didn't like myself. There was something missing, not only from my life but from my insides. But I wasn't ready to look there yet. So, I did what anyone would do, probably what you are doing now when things get uncomfortable or are moving too slowly…I DID MORE STUFF.

Just one more project. And then I heard a still, but powerful voice say to me:

"You know there's an easier way, right?"

I ignored that internal nudge, that inner knowing. I decided that if the recognition I received from being *next to* the famous ones didn't give me satisfaction, I would make myself famous. There, that'll do it.

So I created projects and audacious goals like competing in bodybuilding. I did well too; I placed third in my master's category (for 38+ year olds) and fourth overall. Now I had the perfect muscular flat-bellied body. Everything was set!

Not long after that show, I was on the hunt again, looking for the next transformational breakthrough. As I was planning my next venture, I heard this from somewhere deep within me: *"If you would just let go of what you think you should be doing, I will show you who you should be being."*

Well that's stupid. Who has time to be?? I put that little insight to the side and dug in my heels. The answer couldn't be as simple as that. Let's try harder.

And I did. I tried all the way to December 27, 2014. But I couldn't ignore that gut feeling on the inside: *How can it be so hard for me to be happy, yet so effortless for anyone else? What is wrong with me?*

I didn't get it. I had all the structure of success, but I couldn't fool myself anymore. I was tired of the comparisons and the measuring stick I used to feel good about me. I was tired of losing and winning, and feeling so behind. I needed something different, a new revelation, revolution, an understanding of what I was missing.

And finally…I knew. I knew it was time to surrender.

There was no more tweaking.

No more working.

No more "fixing" my life.

There was nothing I could do to quiet that chatter in my mind and the gentle wisdom in my heart. I had to face what I had been avoiding all these years.

Me.

I had to look at me, the real me inside, to discover why I felt like I couldn't be appreciated or validated unless I was doing something.

I had to face why I felt like my value was only in what I could manifest in front of people.

I had to get real with why I needed to eat and stuff my emotions down in a tight little corner of my heart, and put peanut butter on top so they wouldn't get loose. And that's a big deal, because I will eat anything if it's slathered in peanut butter.

I had to look at me, naked me, and discover her for the first time.

This, dear friend, is the journey you are on. If you are reading this book, you already know. You already feel within you that what you've been doing up to this point is not going to cut it. Maybe it did in the past, and it got you to a successful point. But right now? It's killing you softly as you are coming to terms that your life, your body, your health, and your relationships are suffering because you have not had the courage to face what needs to be faced. Face, feel and heal. This is your work.

This journey is about You. You are about to discover what it means to be big "You" in a little "you" world, where the extraordinary life you create has nothing to do with all that outward stuff you've been taught.

Your magic is about that beautiful essence of Yourself that's been crying to get out from under all that external cover-up. If you think you're awesome now, wait until you meet *Her*. If you think you're crappy now, *She's* going to knock your socks off.

Welcome to the journey of becoming Yourself.

Lori R. Bell

Mariela's Story
NYC, NY

"I had reached a serious crossroads in my career when I began working my way through The Yes Process. I was an elementary school teacher, a job I loved, but it was not my passion. Ever since I can remember I loved acting and singing. Teaching was burning me out both mentally and physically. I wanted to make the transition to being a full time actress but I was AFRAID."

"Because of Lori's coaching, I can now proudly say that I am a full time actress! I am currently represented by 7 agents and have acted in 4 national commercials. I am consistently booking acting, voice-over, and hand modeling jobs about 4 to 5 days a week! I also just joined the Screen Actors Guild (SAG) and started my own LLC. This is the happiest I have ever been in my life and career. I thought being an entrepreneur would be super stressful, but I LOVE it!"

"There are still things on the horizon that I know will make me hesitant and scared but everything is possible with faith. Thank you, Lori, for all your help and your continued support in my journey!"

Phase One
The Awakening

Set the stage for spiritual clarity. Recognize the real power within to remove blockages in receiving and expressing your truth.

CHAPTER ONE
Clearing the Mental Clutter

Having done (and still doing) my own heart work, I know how intimidating The Yes Process can be. I want to come out the gate and tell you something you may not expect, but it is going to please you very well. Before I do, though, I want to say I'm very proud of you. You should be proud of you too. I know what it has taken for you to get to this point.

Lots of emotional bruises.

Some heartache.

Tons of money you've invested.

Endless amounts of time spent researching.

I know this, not only because of my own journey, but because of the journeys of the private clients I coach in my four-month transformation program, called *The Bridge*. Through *The Bridge* training, my clients see the clear path that gets them from where they are in chaos to where they want to be in clarity.

My clients share with me their sacred hopes and dreams and heart desires. Many want to build thriving businesses that reflect their talents and spiritual gifts, but somehow cannot seem to move past "this one thing." *They feel stuck.*

Some clients have strong desires to write a book, sing, or become a designer of something they create and want to mass produce. But every single time they get started they freeze up right in the middle, and many times not far from being finished.

They feel unmotivated.

And perhaps my most frustrated clients are the ones who lay awake at night dreaming of living their calling, their true purpose. They have a vivid imagination of what their dream looks like, and they can see it as easily as you are reading this book. They know they've got what it takes. Everyone around them knows it too, because they hear it from teachers, friends, pastors, and leaders. But their lives are a constant reminder that there is more, and even though they have the passion, they just cannot overcome the blockages to their dreams.

They feel like unleashing their potential in a really significant way.

If you are like my clients who go through my intensive *Bridge* program with me alongside, here is the news that's going to make this all better for you....

The stuck, unmotivated, blocked thoughts and feelings you have? They are the perfect setup for you to launch fully into your calling and your purpose.

This entire book is the real blueprint for how you can transcend perceived limitations and overcome your blockages. What you have really been searching for is not another thing to do. **It is the one thing to be.**

You are dead on target for this launch of your dreams. The only thing you are doing wrong is that you have not fully received your calling because there is so much gunk and junk, a.k.a old programming, in the way.

It's the only thing...but it's THE thing.

You, like my clients and students of TYPU (The Yes Process University), are simply learning how to receive unconditional love. But here's the thing: It's not about loving others. Well, not initially. **It begins with learning how to love YOU.**

When you lack unconditional love of yourself, it *looks like unconditional love of other people.* Practically speaking, it manifests like this:

- Harsh judgement of yourself and others
- Hard-heartedness
- The inability to forgive
- Building walls around yourself
- Punishing yourself and others for not measuring up
- Always busy "fixing" what's wrong in yourself and others
- Lack of gratitude for the blessings already in your life

This is all evidence of a heart that is closed. What you are learning in The Yes Process is how to open your heart to receive the love that you've been withholding from yourself due to the programming that is driving how you think, what you believe, and how you behave.

So what or who taught you you're not good enough or worthy? Usually it's an experience of childhood. And just like streaming a movie into your living room, you are replaying scenes as though it happened yesterday. Now, as an adult you are not only empowered to terminate the streaming movie, but you can create a new one that really serves your ultimate purpose in life.

We are not digging up the tragedies of childhood. We don't have to. They are already present in your right now, because they are the limitations that are causing you to think certain things have to happen a certain way in order for you to achieve the results you are after. You see, you must know the difference between the experience the lesson.

I was working with a woman whom I'll call "Kat" just recently. After years of not dating, Kat met and became very close to her new man. But suddenly, the relationship ended and to Kat it felt like every other time this had happened to her. She could not figure out why, no matter what she tried, where she lived, or where she worked, she kept meeting and falling for the same type of man and getting the same result.

After several minutes during our session, it became clear that Kat was hung up on "when it happened" and "how it hurt her". She was so locked into the pain of the experience that she was missing the whole point of it. I gave her this example.

Imagine your life experiences and lessons to be like your favorite succulent dinner. You order it at a restaurant, and a waiter brings it over. But instead of eating the meal, you start gnawing on the plate!

In reality, when you eat your meal, you *appreciate* the plate on which it is served. Otherwise you would be eating directly off the table. But you don't marvel at the plate so much that you ignore what you ordered. You enjoy your meal, and you thank the waiter for bringing it.

In the great Restaurant of the Universe, your lessons are served up to you via the experiences that have shaped your life. Some have been quite pleasant, and so whenever confronted with a choice, you would certainly choose to have that kind of experience again. But others are heart-wrenchingly painful. Although those are the experiences you would rather avoid, they still make up the total journey of becoming yourself. Instead of taking the lessons, you've held on to the event, replaying every single detail as though it just happened. You are gnawing on the plate.

Do not misunderstand me. I am not minimizing a painful childhood, or glossing over a broken heart. What I am saying is these painful experiences brought you a lesson, and if you don't catch it, you can be stuck right here in depression, sadness, brokenness and fear.

When I'm working one on one, I help my clients recognize that some events helped shape how you see yourself, and therefore how you see the world. And when the way you see yourself and the world has you thinking things only work a certain way for certain people, that is what I call a *mental program*.

So what's the way, or *"The Bridge"* over? The first step to overcoming all of this programming is to unplug from doing so much, driving your life with tasks, to-do lists and the hard energy of just getting things done. You must peel away the things that define who you think you are as a person, in favor of focusing on who you really are as a divine being. It's time to learn how to do things from a place of rest, rather than insecurity.

We're going to shift from the hard outer work of doing, to the inner heart-work of being.

Becoming Yourself

Author and motivational speaker, Denis Waitley said, "it is not who you think you are that holds you back. It is who you think you are not." The process of unlayering and unlearning will begin with this question:

Who are you without all your stuff?

Who are you without your tasks, and your projects and your involvement in this and that?

Who are you without the people and things that have your attention, your time and your energy?

Who are you without sacred beliefs, belief systems, and the thoughts you hold so close?

If you put all these things away, what are you left with?

I'll tell what you are left with. Actually I'll tell you WHO you're left with: YOU. There is nowhere to hide and nowhere to go.

If you are becoming yourself, who is this "self?" The journey begins with knowing who you are without all the stuff you are doing.

Let's look at the difference between doing, being and becoming. The energy of the words and the definitions offer key insights.

Doing means, *"the activities in which a person engages. Effort. Activity. A beating or scolding."* (ouch!)

Being means, *"to have being, to breathe, to draw breath, to be situated, to wait, to linger. Living, being alive, existence."*

Becoming means, *"to begin to be, grow to be, turn into. To qualify or be accepted as; to acquire the status of."*

Can you feel the energy of being as "breathing, waiting and lingering?" Can you feel the flow of "growing to be and turning into?" Can you feel the tension of "effort and activity?" And really, haven't you been beating yourself down and scolding yourself long enough? It doesn't take spiritual enlightenment to see that we have had it backwards all this time. "Being" and "becoming" definitely overcome doing.

Now, let me clarify something. Am I saying that all you have to do is quit your job, dream up something amazing and just "be"?

No. Of course not.

But, what I am pointing you to is focusing on the internal being-ness of discovering yourself and THEN taking INSPIRED action. The doing that you will be...doing...will be from a place of being, FIRST. That means the stuff you think you need to be engaged may not really need your attention. It means if you released the things you think you cannot give up right now, even in some small way, you will free up some white space in your life. Space will provide you room to allow the flow of guidance and clarity that will carry you throughout everyday.

I am leading you home to Yourself. Notice in the definition of "being" is the word "breath." And another word for breath? Spirit. *Pneuma*. The breath of life. When you are not being, you are neglecting the most precious part of who you are. You have become a human doing and have forgotten that you are a *Spirit Being*.

Unplugging: Doing everything from rest

I will let you off the hook. All of this misguided doing has not been your fault. At least not up to the point you finish this book. But for most of your life, it is probably safe to say you have never really learned another way.

Look at what our society teaches us. We are rewarded, heralded and lauded for winning. For most of our entire lives we are competing against peers in order to measure effectiveness and ability. We are told that hard work is rewarded with the win, and the harder the work the sweeter the victory.

"Just do it."
"Winners never quit."
"Go hard or go home."
"If you're not first, you're last."

Ok, that last one is courtesy of Ricky Bobby

from the movie *Talladega Nights* but you get my point. Here is my ultimate suggestion to you: **If you're faced with the choice to go hard or go home, *GO HOME.***

Home. It's where you live, in the center of your being, where you are free to win on your own terms. Winning is not bad nor is it evil. But you will not win in the "competition" of life until you realize there is none. There is just YOU.

This is why The Yes Process is not about fixing. I do not fix any client that is supported in *The Bridge* or any student that enrolls in TYPU Masterclasses. The Yes Process is about uncovering, discovering, unlearning and remembering who you were so you can be that again. We shake off the layers of who we think we are not.

For the remainder of this chapter I will help you know how to see what you have been holding on to and what you can release. I want you to ascend higher into living your dream life and owning your Divinity, meaning your real true identity. This is how I began my journey. By surrendering to doing less so that I can be more and live fully.

When you surrender to doing less, you are learning to conduct your life from a place of rest. Rest means you are refreshed in the doing. There is no anxiousness here. There are no must-do's or have-to's. The action you take throughout your day is inspired and it comes from a joyful peaceful place.

Remember that moment I talked about earlier? When you will come to the end of yourself? This is it, this is the moment. I'm going to help you "seek ye first the kingdom." It is hidden in plain sight. *Hidden in you.*

Truth Seeker, you are being called out now. There

is a call for separation in this season where it is time to draw away from all the external things that are distracting you and into the private chambers of your own inner being.

How to do it all by letting most of it go

Strange contradiction, right? How in the world can you get it all done by not doing it? It's simple, really. **What you think you need to do is most likely a programmed belief you've learned and adopted as truth.**

One of the top three reasons most people do not move forward into living a fully satisfied life is "I don't have time." We have all said this at some point. But I offer this to you, it is not that you do not have time. It is that there is so much other stuff clouding your judgement of what really needs to be accomplished in your day. There is an overwhelming amount of tasks, responsibilities, hobbies, and jobs that compete for any one person's attention. In our fast-paced overstimulated lives it is no wonder it is so difficult to stay motivated to start or finish any purposeful work.

"There is always time to do what matters most," my mentor taught me. We were working together peeling back the layers of my life and I couldn't wrap my mind around why I felt tired, depleted, lethargic and confused when it came to living my true purpose and calling. We took a look at my life and discovered there were thirteen busy-bodied projects that held my creative energy captive, and therefore blocking my flow. I was in everything from a multi-level marketing business to podcasting. I eliminated the distractions by not only unplugging from doing so much, but also analyzing what I was engaging my time, attention, money, emotions, and physical presence.

I like to use the term "unplug", because when you are honest with yourself about your energetic connections, you will see the sources that are powering you up. You will also see what is plugged into you. And your first brave act of The Yes Process is breaking your power connections. This is where you begin the "unlayering" to understand and know just who you are without all your doing. You will also see who other people are when you shut off their power connection to you. It's an eye-opening experience as you learn to stand on your own, in your own power, merrily doing the things that you know you are called to do. You learn that "no" is a complete sentence, and with every no is a hearty YES to becoming more of yourself.

The unplugging process for me lasted several months. Nine months to be exact. I needed that much time to disconnect from mental and religious programs, societal judgements, and anything that was taking me off my divine path. In order to become the real Me, I needed to locate where I was. I had to be analytical about *everything*. I questioned my associations, habits, thoughts, tasks, responsibilities, and relationships. I brought it all under scrutiny, completely deconstructing this thing called "me". In the end, the only activities that survived the cut were the things that were life to me.

I discovered many of the things I was doing were purely out of insecurity ("*I don't like this, but they are depending on me*") or validation ("*If I keep doing this, I will finally matter*"). When I took a hard look at what I was engaged in and why, I clearly saw my energy leaks. Out of thirteen projects and responsibilities I examined, only three of them really lit my fire. The rest were lukewarm desires that were sucking the life right out of me.

Unplugging your life from external power sources teaches you how to operate from a peaceful place of rest. It is the doorway into The Yes Process. Right now, your doing may be out of a lack of self-acceptance or a need for outward validation. The reason you are feeling stuck in your journey is that you have your "do" where your "who" should be!

When you are clear on who you are, there are certain activities you will no longer do. For example, right now you may be feeling insecure about your qualifications to get a new position at work. And every time you feel this, especially in the presence of certain others, you go into panic mode. "*What if they don't see me? What if she gets it and I don't? I better stay later and come in earlier if I want that promotion!*"

So, you will do things that are completely counter to who you are. You'll sign up for activities at work that you HATE. You will put up with attitudes and behaviors that are distasteful and unkind. You will go out of your way to be seen, recognized, heard and acknowledged, sacrificing your home and social life just to get ahead. When all you really have to do is understand who you are in your divine identity, and honor that inner wisdom within you that tells you you are more than enough.

I am working with a client right now who inherited a day care business from a family member. She's been doing it for while now, and while the business is going well, what really lights her up from the inside is not the daycare! But up until we started *The Bridge,* she was suffering her way through it, convincing herself that she was going to just make this thing work. As a result, everyday at work felt like a chore and sometimes an overwhelming responsibility.

Working together, we started unplugging from external sources. We cleared the mental clutter, making way for spiritual clarity. One day during our session, she excitedly told me she received the divine direction she had been seeking all this time. She understood her path clearly and it totally changed her attitude concerning running a business she didn't really want. Today she is preparing an exit strategy for a new owner to run the business while she engages in the passionate work she loves.

When you lead from your inner being, you are establishing your place of power. This is the place of real wealth. It is the well that never runs dry. It means no matter what happens, who goes or who stays, you will be ok. You know who you are. And the way to connecting to that inner power source is unplugging from everything else.

You must align your to-do list with who you are being. If you don't, you will always be chasing the latest and greatest solutions. You want to build your house upon the rock (your real Self), not sinking sand. In fact, when you get into alignment you will find that much of what you have yourself involved in now will change. That to-do list will be shorter as you see just what you can delegate, delete, or design it in a way that fits *who you are.*

So here is your challenge, should you choose to accept it. Commit to a 7-Day Lifestyle Observation, where your only work is to be a witness to your life. I want you to notice what activities, programs, gossip, hobbies, work/job, relationships and other miscellaneous distractions are holding you captive. The goal of this challenge is simply to bring you clarity and understanding of why you do what you do.

When I present this to clients enrolled in The Bridge, almost always they say, "well Lori, I don't do much at all. I go to work/school/church and home." True, you may not be a so-called "busy-body" like I was, but all that means is your distractions are so subtle you are overlooking them. You may not volunteer or sit on every board or committee, but *something* has your precious attention. And as long as you are looking at it, working with it, fussing over it, and being with it, you are ***distracted from looking at YOU.***

Day by day, I want you to be very introspective and very observant. Keep a special notebook for this challenge, because you'll want a record of the life-changing revelations that may surprise you. Visit the book website at www.theyesprocessbook.com where you can receive a day-by-day area of focus to help you get a little structure as you go through this.

Sign up for the challenge at the website (because I want to walk it through with you, just as if you were in The Bridge with me), and you'll get that day's video or audio tip. There are specific instructions I'll have for you for that day only, and you will receive them via your email.

Meanwhile, here are the simplified rules:

1. Make a commitment to yourself that you are open for change and open to see the areas that need an overhaul. After all, change isn't change until you change.

2. Observe your life means notice and *take note*. What gets you upset, excited, happy, joyful, aggravated or peaceful? There are key findings in your reactions to things throughout your day.

3. Everyday choose a focus area. The 7 areas of focus are:

- Workplace/Job (even if you're an entrepreneur)
- Hobbies
- Passions/Dreams
- Relationships
- Projects
- Volunteer Work/Civic duties
- Social Media

4. DO NOT FIX OR JUDGE. Whatever you are aware of is just what it is. With awareness comes the power to choose, so do not say "I do this way too much or not enough." You can change it later. For now, we are just noticing.

5. At the end of 7 days, read over your notes. You should have notes about your feelings, your attitudes, your thoughts. If you were brutally honest with where you are right now, you are empowered to make some hard decisions about what needs to go, stay or change in order to move forward.

The 7-Day Challenge requires you to tap into the feeling you have when you are faced with doing a particular thing. When you go to work everyday, how do you feel? Exasperated? Aggravated? Joyous? Elated? Write it down. In the videos, I'll give you great tips for what to do when your work pays the bills but zaps your energy.

What you'll discover in this Challenge is where you should spend the majority of your time creating and thriving. There are some things that can make your heart sing just thinking about it. I call this "genius work."

I am this way in my coaching practice. I get off the phone with the clients I support and I feel like I could run a marathon! I can be tired doing some things, but when I have a client appointment I get excited. At the end of the call, I literally feel plugged in and turned on!

It wasn't always this way, however. Genius work can be intimidating. Of all things you do, genius work scares you the most. It is what keeps you up at night calling you, because you know *this is what you are supposed to be doing.* And it can also keep you in your head asking the dreaded "how" questions. *How will this work? How can I make money doing this? How will this fit in my life?*

Later I'll show you how to get out of your head and into your heart. For now, just know that genius work items are what you are called to bring forth. This is where your to-do list comes from when you structure your life around what matters most. This is the beginning of learning how to be.

What Now?

Now you have graphic evidence of how well you are really doing (or not) at releasing your creative and spiritual gifts and talents. By your own admission and tally of your busyness, you can clearly see what needs to be eliminated. You are now set up and empowered to make some hard choices. It is time to let go and give notice. And in some cases you don't have to give notice, you can just leave.

At www.theyesprocessbook.com I'll give you some scripts you can use with your inner circle people, your outer circle, and the ones on the perimeter to let them all know you are unplugging from the drama. It doesn't have to be painful, but as you will soon find out, this very important step in The Yes Process is evidence of how much you're willing to love yourself starting here and now. Ultimately, only you can decide what is best for you, but really it boils down to how free do you want to be?

Do not overlook this very simple but powerful Challenge. Before you move forward in The Yes Process, you must have a clear picture of where you are. There is so much supporting you in this bold move forward. Your willingness to quiet the noise and tune into the flow of divine wisdom from within sends a clear signal outward that you are ready to receive the guidance you've been waiting for.

My process of unplugging took 9 months. With my clients, we go deep and surrender to 4 months. For you, the challenge is 7 days to only notice and observe what keeps you off-track. Once you do that, the only thing left is to deal with overcoming the blockages to your success. How? The answers are coming up next, when you discover what to do with all that white space in your life after you let go what is not serving your highest purpose.

CHAPTER TWO
What To Do When You're Not Doing

Your greatest challenge in The Yes Process is **receiving and expressing the real truth of who you are**. What you are here to learn is exactly what you came to teach. That is why what you are going through right now *really is* The Yes Process.

Trying to figure out the "how" parts of this journey is the #1 reason why people cannot say YES. *"I'll say yes when you show me all the steps. I'll say yes when I know the way."* The #2 reason? Old programming that governs self-worth, self-esteem and your outlook about life.

Now, you may be thinking, *"but I am saying yes and I still feel stuck."* I thought I was saying yes too. However, if you have stepped up and out into what you believe is your true calling and you still feel stuck...*your yes has conditions.*

How do you know when you have a conditional yes? If you start something and then somewhere in the middle you change your mind or change your focus? That is a conditional yes. In other words, when you cannot see your way, you stop. So have you really said yes?

When you have a half-hearted conditional yes, your love also has a price tag of conditions. You will judge others by their progress and compare yourself to them. You will withhold your love and become very critical towards the people closest to you, like a spouse or your children, when it concerns their behavior and what they are not doing well.

Saying yes means, *"I don't know the way, but I'm sold out. I'm moving through it."* Many times you HAVE been saying yes. Look at what you have achieved so far in life! You should be extremely proud of the awards you've won and the promotions you've earned. You could not have done those things without at least some form of yes. However, it is at this point that you must *go deep.*

You cannot dip your toe in the water any longer. What got you here will not get you over there. You've said yes to a lot of things. But what is blocking you is that you have not said yes to THE thing.

This is a deeper work that requires you to now say yes to the journey. You've got to stay committed to the vision *even when it looks like it is not working.*

There were many days when The Yes Process looked like it wasn't working. I am talking about as a personal internal work as well as a global platform. There were days I just did not want to show up. But I was sold out. I said yes. I signed up to be a Herald and a Vessel. I had to keep going.

Some of the questions I get from my *Bridge* clients at this stage are, *"If I stop doing some of these things, what will I have left?"* Or, *"If I'm not actively pursuing a goal or a dream, what am I doing when I'm not doing?"* And this is the crux of this whole entire work. **When you stop doing things out of your insecurity, what is left is working on yourself, where you are intentionally creating space for the real message of The Yes Process to come through for you.**

Let me give you my personal example. At the time when I began The Yes Process, I was so sure I knew what it was. I had just completed my first body-building show and I knew I had brilliant insights on how to reach goals and stick with it. So, naturally I assumed The Yes Process was all about saying yes to the goal and the pursuit of it, driving hard and not giving up. Boy was I way off the mark.

Without doing my inner work and actually going through this process myself, I began teaching something that was very motivational and "feel - good", however it was not the real message. Everybody else was teaching it too! My topics were about health and goals, productivity and goals, dreams and…goals. There was no originality and it was not resonating with my audience.

I started a blog, a Facebook page and even a podcast and all of it was about teaching how to make something happen. I grew my Facebook page to just a couple hundred and gained a handful of followers for my podcast. And you know what? It was excruciating hard work. All that effort yielded very little result. The saddest part was it reminded me of all the other times I had tried something and had done ALL that hard work, yet did not get anywhere near the return I deserved.

Any half-decent Google search could reveal anything you want to know about anything. It is not for lack of information that we are not who we want to be. *It is lack of authenticity.*

Let's be real. You already know what to do. **You don't know who to be**, and because many people are not willing to be diligent enough to do their inner work, you do not see a real authentic message. You don't know what a "yes" looks like because there is so much marketplace noise that gives you the outer work of the work. Without doing my heart work, I was one of the ones skimming the surface with information.

I had become so used to trying and failing, and

trying and half-way succeeding that I had created some very interesting programming about what I could really accomplish. My internal programs sounded like this:

• *"Well of course you aren't getting the results you want! You don't know what you're doing."*

• *"So you've met Oprah and you've been on the cover of a national magazine. Big whoop. You did those things with the help of other people. You've never made it on your own."*

• *"You don't have what it takes."*

• *" The truth is, you really are business stupid. There's no way you'll build a real thriving business teaching this."*

• *"Maybe if you had the right mastermind group/coach/ husband/kids/lived in the right area things would be different."*

And on. And on.

I had no idea the damage I was doing in my psyche and the amount of self-loathing that was going on. The more those programs played in the background of my mind, the more I was convinced they were true and real. How could they not be? They popped up every time I was faced with anything, and I had become so used to what I was thinking that by now it was a normal way to think. It was my normal way to be. And this governed my results *in every area of my life.*

It controlled how my relationships worked.

It controlled how much weight I lost (or not).

It controlled they way I parented.

It controlled the way I approached any new goal or task that required me to beat it down and win. I was a mess.

When I took my unplugging challenge, it was an awakening for sure. I remember it like yesterday.

It was the early morning hours of December 27, 2014. As I was making my way to bed several texts and Facebook posts got my attention.

A friend told me to get ready, because her multi-million dollar project was about to kick off. She said expect to see in the new year.

A marketing coach that I had followed since her early days was launching her latest project and suddenly she was *everywhere*.

An acquaintance that I hadn't heard from or seen in about a year had just crossed over 450,000 followers on her Facebook page. Last time we talked she had just launched her brand new coaching business. She had maybe one or two clients at the most.

I was bewildered. Here were concrete examples of people in my world with whom I had either started, or with whom I knew had had some measure of success but nothing major, yet they were exploding on the scene.

And there was little ole me, still puttering along, trying to make it. Something must be wrong with me. I followed all the steps. I subscribed to the right newsletters, bought the guru-programs. But after all this time, I still felt empty.

"I give up," I said out loud.

"On what?", my husband asked.

"On trying so hard. There must be something I'm missing. I don't get it. I know a lot of stuff, yet I'm struggling to really release my potential. There must be something I don't know or maybe I've ignored, but I've got to figure this thing out."

From there, I said the most simple prayer I've ever prayed. "God, if I'm going to be anything in this new year and beyond, you have got to show me what

I'm missing. I don't know what to do anymore. I need help."

And with that, I went to bed.

How to surrender

If you are following this story and nodding in agreement, congratulations! You are well on your way inside The Yes Process. What I did is called surrender. There are three stages of surrender, and you will know where you are when you read the stages.

Stage One: *"I don't know what to do anymore."*

It is interesting to me that as frustrating as it feels to not know what to do, it is also the most liberating! Not knowing what to do (and saying so) is a huge signal to the universe that you are taking your hands off the situation and letting it go. Great! Now you can prepare for the miracle!

I have noticed my kids when they don't know how to do something, especially my five year old. He will announce, "Mommy, can you make me a jelly sandwich?" After I say yes, he runs off, fully expecting it to be done. He has completely surrendered knowing that in the next few minutes he'll have a jelly sandwich on the counter. He knows that he doesn't know how to make the sandwich, and he's happy to let me do what he doesn't know how to do.

Usually you come to this stage after you have done all the steps and all the programs. You have dutifully followed instructions. You have copied, *ahem,* "modeled" the path of others hoping to get the same results they have achieved.

The problem with that is you have no idea what the back story to their success is. You don't know the real-real deal of what that person had to give up in order to be who they are today. Right here is literally the point at which The Bridge clients find me. They have exhausted the options. They do not know what to do anymore.

Stage Two: *"I need help."*

I did not know what I was doing. I did know that whatever it was, I was doing it wrong. This is the second part of surrender. Asking for help. I say this all the time in The Yes Process that **you cannot become Yourself by yourself.** Because the truth is, if you knew what to do you would be doing it!

In the early days of my "pre-client" (because I believe in my work so much, everyone who calls is a pre-client) intake process, I offered free 20-minute strategy sessions. Big mistake. I quickly found that a person who was struggling with her inner programing was not signing up to work with me. She was calling for a free coaching session. She wanted to get out of her mess, and she did NOT want a program! What she was basically saying is, *"I need help, but I'm willing to suffer a little longer, keep looking, and tweak this thing on my own."*

If you find yourself a coach or mentor and you feel like you could work with them, *"but"*…you are not at surrender yet. You've got to know, if you ask for help be open to receiving it, no matter what that help looks like. I know I am called to serve women who are ready.

Today, instead of offering free strategy, I offer Discovery Sessions. This takes the pressure off everyone; I'm not selling anything and the pre-client doesn't have to feel pressured to buy anything.

My point is, at this stage, when you ask for help be ready to receive. Expect the help and don't waste a moment on trying to tweak something just a little more. Know that what you've prayed for is already here. This leads us to the next stage of surrender…

Stage Three: *"I went to bed."*

Yep. That's right. Go to bed. Read a book. Go play. Go anywhere and do anything that takes your mind off your request. Having fun and feeling good puts you in receive mode. As long as you're thinking about what you don't have, or what is not yet manifested, you are in a lack mentality where nothing exists. No thing.

Like I mentioned earlier, when my son asks for a jelly sandwich and I say yes, he runs away to go do something that occupies him while he is waiting. Usually that means a nice sprint through the house or some super hero mega Lego war with his brother. But either way, he is not thinking about the fact that he is not yet eating a sandwich. He is off having fun and loving life.

We can learn so much about life paying attention to kids. Learn to play like a child. Have fun in your waiting!

The art of receiving

We are now moving into the meat of the heart work that is required in The Yes Process. We must learn the art of receiving.

After you learn how to truly surrender, you are now wide open to receive. This is what you're doing when you're not doing the stuff that has distracted you. This is the real work that you should be engaging! It's not that stuff that is constantly filling your to-do lists. On the journey of becoming yourself you are learning how to "cease striving", as the Bible says in Psalm 46:10. You are making room now for clarity to come through.

Receiving is indeed an art. On the other end of asking is receiving. The transfer is not complete until this happens! By definition, to receive means *"to be sent, be given, be told, to experience."* This is all action, but it is not the action of the giver. It is *your action* that completes the cycle. So if you do not have what you have been praying for, what is happening between asking and receiving?

Before we answer that question, we've got to understand the flow of information, or *energy*, how it comes and where it comes from. I promise you that if you learn this, you will never again say words like "I don't know" or "I feel stuck". I am about to equip you with a powerful truth that will set you free in your asking and your receiving.

Here's why what you see is what you get

If there is something in your life you desire but have not manifested yet, it is because the thing you asked for is at a level of energetic vibration to which you have not attuned yourself. In other words, you cannot ask for a million dollars and have a secret belief that you are only worth a thousand.

You can pray for a million dollar business, but it will require a million dollar mindset and million dollar habits. Your blessings will not meet you at the level of your mess. You must rise to meet them, and to do that you must first understand the flow of energy, and then how this flow is blocked by your inability to receive.

Understanding the flow of divine energy

Humans are all spirit beings. This means that at our core, we are pure energy. It has been proven through quantum physics that all things in this material universe is made of energy. Our bodies are made of atoms and subatomic particles and if you examine these to the nth degree you will see these are made of energy waves.

We are not only a creation of spiritual substance, we are Spirit. We are an extension of this Presence that many call God in human form. You can think of this human form as a shell.

The creation story as recorded in the Bible says a key verse that illuminates this spirit-connection. In Genesis 1:26 it is written that God said "let Us make man in Our image and after our likeness." The word "God" is from the Hebrew word "Elohim" which means *"gods, goddesses, and god-like ones."* The "Elohim" of creation created humans in the energetic likeness, image, and design to be representatives of this power and presence.

As extensions of this God-Presence, we are here in this material earth realm to express the glory, the beauty and the magnificence of who we really are. God is Spirit, and although we have been trained to believe "He" is a he, "He" is genderless Spirit. God is known by many names but I believe God is presence and love. I like to say Presence or Love because it gives your mind nothing to imagine or conjure. Presence or Love has no face, only energetic vibration and *you'll know what it is by the way you feel.*

I discovered the four levels of the subconscious mind through a book called *The Power of Self* by Kim Michaels. I definitely recommend reading his book if you want further, deeper study on the workings of energy. For our purposes here, I'm going to explain it as it relates to The Yes Process.

Your mind operates in four dimensions, or levels. The levels are the "hierarchy" so to speak of how and why energy flows through you the way it does. Understanding these levels will help you quickly recognize why you are not getting the results that you have been praying for.

The first dimension is **Identity**. This is the highest level of the subconscious mind. This is where your basic sense of identity is stored. It is your name, nationality, race or family. Not only that, but here you hold the deeper beliefs about what kind of being you are, how you relate to the world in which you live, and what your abilities and limitations are. *It is the "big picture"* of your life.

The second dimension is **Thought**. Thoughts are determined by your sense of identity. They can be changed, shared and formed. *Thoughts are what you think about the big picture.* They help you understand the details of the big picture. A thought is simply an idea and cannot of itself lead to an action. In order to be translated into action a thought needs one very necessary component of this next third level.

The third dimension is the realm of **Emotion.** This is the seat of your feelings. Emotions determine *how you feel about the big picture*, yourself and the world. Emotions dictate how the thoughts you are thinking are acted upon.

The final dimension is the realm of **Matter**. It is in this realm that what you see is what you get. This is the physical manifestation of what's been going on in the background, and this is where most people are conditioned to pay the most attention. The realm of Matter is your body and all outward representations. This is the place where feelings have fueled the thoughts shaped by identity and are now acted upon.

Pulling all of this together, remember, I said we are spirit beings, extensions of Elohim. Our human bodies are merely manifestations of our divine selves in this earth realm, or "matter."

There is a continuous stream of energy flowing from your Source into you. And every time you have a desire for something, or you pray for something to happen in your life, the answer is immediately translated into you through these four dimensions.

The reason it feels like your prayers are never answered, or are extremely slow to be answered is because pure Source Energy flows first through your identity. If your sense of identity, or who you believe you are, is imperfect and clouded by your experiences, you are not receiving a clear transmission. Based on who you believe you are, you will think certain thoughts. From there, you'll feel some way about the thing you have asked, and when all three of these are working together, you will produce the results you have been getting!

When I share this with *The Bridge* clients, it is like a major lightbulb moment here. They can easily see why if they have been thinking and feeling a certain way nothing they will ever do from the outside will ever work. If you are like my clients, you have been trying to change the physical realm without working on the inside!

Here is an example that will show you how this looks in real life. With my clients, I take something they really want to overcome and lay it out plainly. In just a few minutes they will see the clear path to why things have not been working they way they want. Here's a common example.

Imagine you are overweight and you are ready to get it together. This time you want to do this thing for real. You put everything you've got into it. So you pray for an answer. The pure God-energy, the Light of Love is immediately released. When it is released it is untainted, unblemished and perfect. But when released into a mind with an imperfect view of itself it looks like this:

- Your answer shows up in the form of a diet and exercise plan. This is something that's not quick-fix, you know it will get you results when you work it. You start off so excited! But 3 weeks in, your enthusiasm is waning. Everything is so hard for you. (**Identity**)
- You try harder to stick with it. You don't think you can do it. After all, nothing you've ever tried really worked anyway. Why do other people have it so easy? (**Thought**)
- You start feeling depressed and sad. You really thought this time was it. All the money you've spent! All the promises and guarantees that diet made! You begin to feel sad as you know you really suck at this. (**Emotion**)
- You step on the scale and of course, you've gained back 2 of the 5 pounds you lost when you started. What a failure you must be! (**Matter**)

What a vicious and unfair cycle! Why didn't you know this before? You could have been fixed a long time ago! It's ok though, don't beat yourself up. This is why you're reading this book! There is an easier way to transform your life, but you've got to do the heart-work you signed up for.

This is why The Yes Process is the journey of becoming yourself. And it is also why I tell pre-clients you cannot become yourself by yourself. Sometimes you just don't know what you don't know.

When you understand that nothing is "wrong" with you, and that you just have an imperfect view of who you are, you are empowered to make some new choices. But trying to change your situation from the outside realm of Matter is like fixing your car engine by changing the tires.

The heart of the, "matter", is an inside job of surrendering and letting go so that you can learn the real truth of who you are. When you do that, the person you really are is going to astound you with her capabilities. You can truly become a powerful conscious creator of your reality. But you must know who you are.

Now a new question arises. It is not only about getting better results now, because you have clearly been doing all the right work. The next logical step in this process is what my clients all want to know: "*How do I change my perception of myself?*" The answer is simple, though not always easy.

In my sessions with clients of *The Bridge*, we do proprietary work that helps them change the way they see themselves. We have all heard that if you "change your thoughts you can change your life." I believe this is true to a point. As you can see, changing your thoughts is only a beginning step.

If you really want to change your life, you must begin by changing your perception of yourself. You must start at the level of your identity.

This leads us to the next phase of The Yes Process where you begin walking in the pure light of the truth of who you really are. It is the place where you've got to give it all up, everything you think you know and follow the path of Truth, no matter where it leads.

Ashley's Story
Columbia, SC

"Before meeting Lori and being introduced to The Yes Process, my life was in a place of stagnation and frustration. I knew the vision that God had given me but I had no clue how to execute it. I had no framework and while I knew I needed to move forward I had no sense of direction."

"I reached out to Lori, as I was inspired by her personal testimony and journey. As a result of implementing Lori's system, I have now established my organization, moved forward in gaining our 501 C-3 Status and ready to implement our first program!"

"The Yes Process continues to teach me how to utilize the resources God has set before me, value each season my journey takes me, and more importantly realize that God is my source for everything. I am challenged to say Yes to every area in my life while relinquishing the fear of success!"

Phase Two
Divine Recovery

Learn your divine identity and how to use the power of your identity to transcend human limitations. Learn how to go within for the authentic truth of who you are.

CHAPTER THREE
Enter the Cave, Find the Treasure

I paint a vivid picture in my head about this path. Up to this point we have been clearing away the thick, dense brush to reveal the path of truth. I imagine you and I are walking together through the emotional jungle surrounding your life, and using the machete of The Yes Process, we are clearing the way and making room for spiritual clarity. And just when you think it's about to be over, here we are at what I call **"The Cave."**

I was speaking with a client, whom I'll call "N" last week about this analogy. N was excited about the progress she had made, we both were, but then she was faced with entering The Cave. We had cleared the path. Now it was time to overcome the issues that attracted her to The Yes Process in the first place.

It was a place N had never been before, and as we were moving forward I could sense her fear and hesitation.

"I don't like this Lori," she said. "I don't like feeling like this and being this vulnerable." I felt such compassion because I had felt the same rage of emotions myself. "I know you don't," I reassured her. "You've never been this way. And the best part about this moment right now is that you don't have to do it alone." And with that, we went in.

The Cave, as I see it, is that deep dark emotional place that is within all of us but we'd rather not see it. Wait, see it? I mean not talk about it. In fact we would rather not even acknowledge it, convincing ourselves that the less we bring it up the more it will stay buried.

No. It does not work that way.

The Cave houses the places within us that are so wounded it feels better to just let it alone. It's like the fight club no one wants to talk about. We avoid talking about it by doing all the things that it takes in order to not "go there."

That's where to-do lists come from. Staying busy and calling it productive. Tending to everyone else's business and engaging in everyone else's process helps keep you distracted just long enough to forget that you have festering wounds.

Being plugged-in to social media, news media and every controversial subject that society thinks needs your attention is a great way to stay actively uninvolved in what really needs your attention. It's the overgrown elephant in your private emotional room.

Unfortunately, issues do not stay hidden and open wounds get infected. They show themselves at the time you are least likely to want to deal with them! And The Cave is where they are buried.

Here's the good news: You are not alone. You may not be a *Bridge* client (yet!), but you are here connecting with me through this book. We are going in together.

Here's the better news: You are equipped to go inside The Cave. I am your guide and I'm holding the Light.

Here's the <u>best</u> news ever: YOU are the Light! All you have to do is look in the direction of the darkness and illuminate. There is nothing to conquer, nothing to kill. Just stuff to face, feel and heal.

See? It's not as scary in there as you think.

If we are going through The Cave together, there is one thing on which you must be clear. This is a path of truth. Nothing will be left to chance. You must determine for yourself that you will follow the path of truth no matter where it leads.

Truth does not compromise.

Truth does not discriminate.

Surprisingly, truth rarely looks like your expectations.

We're going in.

Following the path of Truth

Knowing where to look is a tricky situation. Because in your human mind there are some things of which you are pretty sure certain. But it is this level of familiarity you must release if you really want to know the truth of things.

If you hold certain beliefs sacred and untouchable, this will be the first area to release. Why? Because these beliefs about yourself, the world, and everything concerning you have clouded your identity. When divine inspiration is released to you, it is met with all that stuff you have believed about you that may or may not be true. Sacred beliefs hold special influence for you because they tell you what to think, how to behave, and who to be. They are your navigational system.

The problem with sacred beliefs is that they did not come from You. Not the real You. Not your Sacred Divine Self. They are a form of the truth which you have not truly experienced for yourself. Like recipes handed down through generations, your beliefs are the stuff of hopes and dreams, and fears and doubts.

Who are you without your beliefs? Where are your boundaries? What would you do with yourself if you did not have a certain code to live by that kept your world in a nice, neat little orderly box?

Have you ever thought to yourself, *"what have I been believing that has guided my life to this point?"* It's an important question, and you will need courage to explore the answer. You must be willing to strip down, to the bare naked nothingness of zero, in order that you can be filled with the eternal truth of Love.

When I began my journey, I prayed a dangerous prayer. I asked for truth to be revealed to me. I did not know what I was asking for. I just wanted the emotional bleeding to stop. I wanted to find out why I felt so stuck, behind everyone else, and unworthy. I was so scared of myself, and it wasn't the fear of doing something that scared me. I was good at doing. I was terrified of NOT doing something. The thought of never fulfilling my own big potential kept me up at night. I was ready for change.

The answer to my prayer was found in silence for me. I felt within me the subtle thoughts of Love that seemed to bubble up from the inside and said, *"If you want truth, that is what you'll find. But you must follow the path no matter where it leads."*

Uh-oh. I did not know what I was in for.

I told God that I did not want a religious truth. I knew the Christian side of things, because I was born and raised in it. I know the story of Jesus and I had accepted salvation as a teen. I know divine healing, speaking in tongues, tithing, and church. Yet I still felt like there was something deeper than what I was being taught. It was like accepting a gift, but not realizing there was an entire storehouse where that one came from.

In your mind you already have an idea of what and where "truth" is. After all, it is your truth that has gotten you this far. Whether that is a good thing or not, it has reaped you the results you have now. If you are reading this book, you know there is more truth, or at least something deeper to discover.

If you grew up religious, as I did, truth means Jesus and everything in the Bible. And this is where The Yes Process began for me.

I did not know that I had an issue with my Christian beliefs. Looking back on it now, I see that I started getting curious about religion and religious teaching somewhere around 2014. But overall, I was happy in Jesus. Until the day came when I started asking questions.

Oh my. The questions.

The shift really did hit the fan.

Remember when I said you cannot become yourself by yourself? Well, I didn't. I was led by inspiration to my mentor who had walked a similar path that I was undertaking. I did not have expectations, other than to be free to be me. The real me, without the labels and everything attached to my outside identity. Labels only served to define who I am, what I believe, and who my friends are.

It was during this time Pandora's box opened. The guidance I was receiving from within constantly was, *"You asked for truth. Follow the path."* The path led me straight to the deep, dark cave of religion.

I did not expect nor intend for my beliefs about God, Jesus, the Bible, and the church to be examined. It was all I knew and to mess with that foundation was to mess with the very core of who I am.

Freedom from religious bondage was not what I asked for, but it was exactly what I needed and the journey has not been easy. It was scary, uncertain and lonely. I lost some friends and affiliations. Some family members told me I was certainly hell-bound and could not support me on this path.

It hurt, but I understood. I did not ask anyone to join me where I was going, because this is the kind of journey that you walk for yourself. This is not a "take a friend" along for the ride. This is a one-way ticket to spiritual truth and understanding and one that you can only know by experience.

Religion may not be part of your sacred code, but I bet there is something that you are holding on to that you believe will save you by keeping it, or kill you by letting go.

You must understand that the treasure you seek is in The Cave. It's deep. It's dark from years of neglect and cover- up. It looks way too scary, but only because you've ignored it for so long. However, it is in the deep places of your heart, the parts that scare you the most, that is where you will find what you have been searching for all this time.

Freedom.

Love.

Peace.

Liberation.

Wealth.

Truth.

Identity.

You only need to surrender your beliefs and learn to question it all. When you think about it, all that you know about yourself is what someone else told you. Do you know who you are? If the first thing that pops up for you is your name, your nationality, your race or your religion, you do not have a pure idea of your true identity.

I grew up in a Christian family, in a Christian community, and a largely Christian nation. There is no surprise what I thought was right for me, because everyone around me was the same. But through The

Yes Process, I un-layered and un-learned my way back home to Myself.

Go through your Cave. What is waiting on the other side is the person you were born to be in this material realm.

CHAPTER FOUR
Coming Out of the Spiritual Closet

You began this journey searching for Truth. Why is your life working the way it is? What are you not seeing? What needs to be released? These are the questions of the Truth Seeker, the one who is willing to walk this path, obedient to divine instruction, and diligent to carry them out. You are a very special kind indeed.

Since we are at The Cave, may as well go on in, shall we?

You can never lose your divine connection. But you can dismiss it, ignore it, or simply forget it. Sometimes you can allow distraction of what is going on in the world (those energy leaks) to interrupt your awareness of who you are.

You can stay aware by incorporating the same spiritual practice I teach my private clients enrolled in *The Bridge*. I want to show you how to come out of the spiritual closet by doing what I call raise your FLAG and play your CARDs.

If you are feeling things like frustration, fear, anger, confusion, cluttered thinking, depression, sadness or any other low-level emotion or state, this can actually work in your favor. **They are very clear indicators that you are thinking or feeling something that is in direct opposition to what your Source within you is thinking or feeling.**

That is why it is so important to keep watch over Your energy and plug the leaks. You cannot be a powerful vessel when You're leaking. FLAG and CARD methods are easy, great ways to keep your awareness of your alignment to your Higher Self, God within.

The FLAG and CARD techniques, just like all my programs, were intuitively, prophetically received. The inspiration to create these things hits me so hard because I am my own best student first. The FLAG and CARD guidance was born out of my own difficult time learning how to receive the truth and letting go of what I thought I needed to be whole. I remember the day I was led to make these practices part of my daily routine, and teach them in The Bridge transformation programs.

I was seeing some success online with The Yes Process but I couldn't shake this nagging feeling that I was hiding from something.

I was creating videos for my Facebook page, growing my list and felt like I was showing up big. But there was one little area that was still a tender spot of hurt. It's The Cave at its best.

I was slowly coming into the truth of who I really am and the purpose I needed to fulfill with The Yes Process. It was the truth revealed to me concerning the religion that had shaped my whole life.

Letting go of tradition and heritage is extremely difficult. The attachment to what I believed was incredibly strong. You may be feeling the struggle right now. There is a profound truth that is resonating within you, but where do you go with this? How can you come out of the spiritual closet and live the truth you know from within?

It's like a tug-of-war from the inside. I didn't feel safe to be me. Who will believe me? How can I go against what I've learned from my parents and the church? No one I knew in my circle was saying the things that I was thinking. Surely I was crazy. You know what they do with crazy people.

Crazy, unconventionally thinking people are

ostracized.

Crazy independent thinkers are considered blasphemous and heretic.

Crazy truth-seeking spiritual people have missed the mark and were flirting with the devil.

Saying out loud what I knew I was learning through my spirit was risky business. I didn't want to go to hell! And every piece of guidance I got from trusted mentors, friends and advisors said "*do not go there.*" In my corner of the world, I couldn't find anyone to agree with me that it was ok to ask questions and seek answers. Every Christian in my life said I was in demonic territory.

What was everyone so afraid of? What was on the other side of all these questions? Jesus was questioned all the time and encouraged them. But why was everyone so skittish about my personal search?

It is disturbing for people when you start moving in a direction that is opposite where they are headed. One thing is for sure. As you walk this path, you will soon find out what your relationships are made of. If your own spiritual-seeking to become yourself jeopardizes your position, standing, or authority, it might not have been such a strong foundation to begin with.

So what's a person to do? Either you turn tail and run, or you keep following that inner guidance. And I couldn't resist it any longer. I had to know why I was hiding, because it was not immediately obvious to me.

I did the only thing I knew to do. I shut out the noise and went within myself. The kingdom of heaven is within. If you seek it first, everything else will be added to you. I like that kind of math.

This is exactly what you must do if you are

facing the crossroads of believing and moving forward or going back to the way things were. And side note, going back is not even an option. You know too much now. Oops. It is too late. So actually your options are to hang out in divine recovery for the rest of your life and settle for mediocrity, or move forward in faith.

I did not immediately know what the block was, but I was not willing to settle for mediocre success. The conversation went like this:

> **Me**: I'm scared.
> **Spirit**: *Why?*
> **Me**: I'm afraid they will find out. I don't want to be judged by everybody.
> **Spirit**: *Why are you afraid of judgement?*
> **Me**: Because if they really see me they'll run.
> **Spirit**: *Why?*
> **Me:** Because sometimes I want to run from this!
> **Spirit**: *Why do you want to run?*
> **Me:** Because maybe I'm right. And if I'm right, then they're wrong and everything will crumble and it will be all my fault.
> **Spirit**: *What else has been "your fault."*

I drew blank here. I could not think of anything, so I waited. And then slowly, distant memories floated to the surface.

- I was a Captain in the USAF. My boss offered me the chance to lead a very challenging but very visible and highly promotable job. I was so terrified I would screw it up I quickly turned it down. I was used to making wrong decisions and I learned all my life that I cannot be trusted to make important decisions and have people depend on me.

- Before that, there was the time I was in college and was leading a problem-solving debate team. I made a crucial wrong decision that cost of us the match.
- Before that, I was in high school and the coach put me in to pitch since I did it so well in practice. It was my first time. It didn't take long to freeze up and within the first inning I had walked at least 3 people.
- Before that, I was in middle school and missed the basket and we lost the game.

And on and on my history unfolded in my mind all the times I was trusted to do well, support the team, lead from the front and I had fouled it up.

Granted, no one died. But every time I doubted myself based on past experience, *I died*. I was killing my own expression of creativity and brilliance. My mental programs would not let me get close enough to succeed, so I surely wasn't going to fail. I settled for average and being a face in the crowd.

Religion didn't help this mentality. Religion said *"God has an amazing plan for your life. All you have to do is say this prayer and accept his son and you can have the plan."* It was all very conditional, yet I was taught that God's love was unconditional. Such a blatant contradiction, but no one I knew was questioning it.

Growing up, I would sit in church and look at the same people come to Jesus every Sunday with the same issue. We pay our money. We say our prayers. We faithfully attend. Yet none of that brought me any closer to an experience of the true God.

To me, God seemed to work for certain people sometimes. What makes God move? Why did my daddy die of cancer but another person was healed? What kind of temperamental God is this? I was taught never to doubt God, nor question his ways of doing things. But I knew from somewhere deep that maybe I had misinterpreted and misunderstood God.

As I laid these past scenarios out in my journaling, I knew I didn't want this anymore. It was too heavy. It was time to release. My guidance was so clear:

> **Spirit:** *Just let go. You've been hiding beneath all of that old data and programming. They don't even belong to you. Under all that stuff, is who you really are. All you need to do now is raise your FLAG and play your CARDs.*
>
> **Me**: Um. Raise my what now?
>
> **Spirit:** *Raise your FLAG. Play your CARDs. The real work of The Yes Process is found in...*
> *self-**F**orgiveness*
> *self-**L**ove,*
> *self-**A**cceptance and*
> ***G**ratitude.*
> *While doing this,*
> ***C**lear your programs so you can*
> ***A**sk,*
> ***R**eceive and*
> ***D**o.*

Obviously, being in the closet about anything is a metaphor for hiding from the truth. It is the truth of who you are, the truth of what you know and the truth that will set you free.

You can hide and do it well. But while you are hiding in the shadows to protect yourself from hurt and pain, you are also holding from yourself Love. Excitement. The joy of living life in all its fullness!

When you come out of the closet, it begins with

being honest with yourself. If you cannot say "this is me and I stand by her first", you are in the closet.

Spiritually speaking, you cannot move forward in your calling and divine purpose when you cannot be honest with why things are the way they are. It is time to stop hiding. It is time to get real and authentic... *with you*.

This is the key to coming out of the spiritual closet. In the next chapter I am going to walk you through the simple but very powerful techniques to learn to love yourself, forgive yourself, accept who you are and what you came to do, and be grateful for it all.

CHAPTER FIVE
How to Raise Your FLAG and Play Your CARDs

Raising my FLAG has become a cornerstone practice as I walk people through The Bridge transformations. It has taught me and my clients how to receive solutions to problems, and how to align our lives by either quantum leaping, or bit by bit releasing until we come into full and complete alignment. Playing my CARDs is what allows me to ask big and receive big. It helps take inspired action from a spirit place, and not from insecure trying-to-make-something happen reactions.

The only thing blocking true brilliance and complete access to that place within you where nothing and everything exists at the same time is all the stories you tell yourself about how life is supposed to be. We place so much emphasis on what we did not forgive ourselves for and what happened back way back when.

Unless you clear the distractions and face the mental programs that keep replaying as negative experiences in your life, you will continue to get a false view of who you are. I call this an *illusion* because what you're seeing is not how things really are. It's how *you are*. When you get a clearer picture, you will receive YOUR truth.

This is important. Your truth is what has been revealed to YOU by the Spirit. Remember, when you ask, you always receive because you are directly connected to the Divine. When that energy is released into you it is passed through the dimensions of the subconscious mind. If you do not have a holy concept of who you really are as a spirit being, the divine inspiration you receive is filtered through all the memories of your experiences and ultimately creates your life.

But when you work on yourself and your self-image by going through the cave, there is a level of clarity that you will experience and as a result, you will know the truth. Not only will it set you free, you will learn that you have *always* been free.

How to raise your FLAG

Self-Forgiveness. *"I know it happened so long ago. But I just can't forgive myself for what I allowed."* I have heard this time and again. There are thoughts you transcend, and then there are core beliefs you *dismantle*. A core belief is the root of what you believe about your identity. It is central to *everything* about you. Fear of never reaching your full potential actually comes from the core belief that you are unworthy and not good enough. You can transcend that, either by changing the story or gathering the lessons that experiences were designed to teach you.

When something happens to you that you don't quite understand, your mind creates a story around that event to help reconcile it for you. It is like in school when the teacher would half-way erase the board. Or when you watch the news and they say your personal information is at risk because of this one setting you haven't changed on your phone. If you stay tuned they'll tell you what it is.

These are incomplete events. You simply *must* know know the end of the story! The teacher is never going to keep your attention as long as that spot is on the whiteboard!

Your mind is very clever at protecting you from danger and keeping you from situations that are hurtful. Unfortunately, when you get locked in on certain experiences, the mind does not forget. So when you try to venture out of your zone of comfort, it will snatch you back and "re-mind" you that "un-uh, you remember what happened last time?"

Burning your hand on a hot stove does not mean all stoves are bad and cannot be trusted, right? You see, you know this about stoves. But somehow you lose this realization where relationships are concerned. If your heart was broken on the playground in third grade by a group of girls whom you thought were your friends, your mind created a story behind that. *Girls are so catty and petty. They cannot be trusted. Boys are way easier to befriend.*

Remember I said earlier that childhood experiences and events of your past are set up to teach you valuable lessons about life. But you can get so locked into the *experience* and forget that there was ever a lesson in the first place! And you hold yourself hostage to an experience that was never designed to stay with you forever.

When you learn the lesson you don't need the experience anymore. Imagine a toddler who is now potty-trained. They no longer need the experience of a diaper. They learn the lesson of feeling the sensations in the body when it is time to go to the bathroom. Once the lesson is learned all else is released.

Experiences that stay too long in your consciousness turn to core beliefs in your subconscious. It is like the background music, the soundtrack of your life. They are just under the surface, and depending on the depth of the hurt, they can stay for years, a constant reminder of what happened "last time." Negative core beliefs keep you stuck and confined to this small, limited view of who you are and what you can do. **Self-forgiveness is the key to liberation.**

You did not know what you did not know.

You are divine, but having a human experience. Things hurt. You are not perfect. We are all learning how to live this life. You are no exception.

"But I did know, Lori! I knew better and I did it anyway." Then you did not know. You have head knowledge but your knowing must come from the deeper place of spirit.

You must *immerse* yourself in self-forgiveness. Every moment. Everyday. For EVERYTHING.

Forgive yourself for not knowing.

Forgive yourself for not caring.

Forgive yourself for the neglect of Self and depending on others for happiness.

You are so worthy of Yourself! The experiences were emotionally hurtful but you can now transcend those experiences because you can rewrite your own story.

A few years ago, a friendship ended between me and woman whom I loved. It was abrupt. It was final. I was hurt. I said some things out of insecurity, my own subconscious programming, and it was all she needed to just end it. For two years, I was angry. I wanted an apology and I wanted to apologize. At the very least I wanted a meaningful ending to a relationship that was important to me.

Her apology never came. Neither did mine. And I beat myself about it everyday.

If only I had known what was going on, I would

not have said what I said.

If only she was patient enough with me to let me grow through my own crap and be there for her.

If only I wasn't so insecure about what I meant to her and to us, I would not have said stupid stuff.

And on and on.

Then one day, I settled it. I simply changed the story. I wrote it down and said pieces of it everyday every time my thoughts took me there.

"Lori, you did the best you could with where you were. You truly didn't know your own power. And honestly, neither did she. You said what you said because that was all you knew. And she responded the best way she knew how. You needed each other for that season, and you served each other well. You both loved well from the best place you could, and because of it, you have learned valuable lessons in how to be a good friend."

That's it. It was over. I did not need to keep replaying that situation in a way that makes me look so weak, or make her seem so heartless. I forgave myself for anything that came to mind concerning that time and I was finally ready and able to move on. Now when I think of her, it is with love and appreciation of what she came to teach me.

You say you still cannot forgive yourself for allowing something traumatic to happen to yourself or to someone else. Maybe you were the one to hurt another. It doesn't matter. Forgiveness is forgiveness. If you can extend any measure of forgiveness to anyone else, that same energy, that same vibration of forgiveness is available for you. Just turn the feeling inward and point it at yourself.

Self-Forgiveness is liberating. It is compassionate. And it leads to the one thing we need more of in this world.

Self-Love. MMM-mmm, self-love is the

delicious way to honor who you are in every way, and forgiveness points the way here. There is a physical act of self-love, and we'll get to that in a second, but first, let's talk about the spiritual practice of loving you.

Loving yourself allows you to be gentle with yourself. This is a learning, growing, stretching process. Self-love is like a journey within a journey. We are not taught that it is ok to say "no" when you mean "no", without caveat or explanation. Self-love is not selfish. **It is the most loving thing you can do for this entire planet.**

Think about it. Can one hurt another if they love themselves? You've probably heard the expression "hurting people, hurt people." It is a simple way to explain that the reason someone would bring harm to someone else, is because that person does not love themselves. And when a person does not love herself completely, she cannot love you.

You can tell an unloving person by their speech when they talk about their fat gut and their big butt. You can tell it in the way they go out into the world looking raggedy or unkempt. A person who loves themselves honors their appearance, they don't say horrible things about themselves, and they take life with a healthy dose of grace.

Nothing escapes love. Love covers and overcomes everything, including mistakes and errors. If you live in the light of your own love, everything you go through in this world would never be an issue for you, for everything will be motivated by love.

In the material physical realm, self-love looks like kindness toward yourself. Knowing not only your worth, but that you are worthy. Appreciating your own inner beauty. It's patience with mistakes and loving yourself through them.

I remember when my children were learning to walk. Each one went through the stages of being mobile, from scooting on their belly to pulling up and supporting on furniture. They would take a step and fall down. My middle son simply could not be persuaded to walk. In fact he would take a step or two, and if he caught you looking he would just sit down. So we left him alone and one day he "let us" catch him walking and he kept on going.

Not one time during their learning-to-walk stage did I scold them for falling down. Not once. Never did I say, "Really? You're 13 months old now. You don't have this figured out yet? How dumb are you?!" But I can remember specific times in my personal development that I reprimanded, scolded, chided and nearly cussed my own self out because I hadn't "figured it out" yet!

I was working with a woman in The Bridge program who was used to messing things up and not getting it right. She would say things like, "I should know this by now." Or, "I've heard this before. Why can't I remember how to do this?!" She was incredibly hard on herself. In our first session I would constantly remind her and repeat, "Be extremely gentle with yourself. You don't know this way. It's a new way to be, so of course you don't know it."

How many times have you said things like that to yourself? How many times have you refused compliments because saying "thank you" is so hard that you feel you need to deflect and say something degrading about who you are? When you are not self-loving you are self-loathing, and it is killing you slowly. Self-loathing teaches you not to trust your decisions, your choices, or your intuition and it's a slippery slope into low self-worth.

True story.

And it looks like this:

- Constant criticizing and scolding yourself
- Overeating
- Believing you are unlovable
- Disorder or disorganization in your environment
- Ignoring your inner guidance
- Speaking unkindly to yourself or about yourself to others
- Bullying or manipulating other people, including your children
- Believing that if your spouse or a loved one has a bad day or is upset in some way, it could be your fault
- When someone refuses a gift or favor from you, or gives you any type of criticism you take it as a personal insult
- Not feeling or believing you are worthy
- If a relationship ends or fractures in any way, you believe it is because you are not worthy of it

If you do any of these things on a regular basis you are self-loathing. So stop it. Here's how.

Saturate yourself, and I mean *saturate yourself,* in loving-kindness toward you. I am talking if a thought creeps in saying, *"well that was stupid"*, you cut it off immediately with, *"well I could've done that differently. I'll do it better next time."* Or something kin to that. **In every moment, get on your own team, and start the day that way.**

When I was really struggling to love who I am, not just what I look like, I came across a talk given by famed inspirational speaker, coach and teacher in the movie *The Secret*, Lisa Nichols. Her life story is a blueprint in triumph. The following exercise was inspired by something she teaches that helps you get on your own team.

Every morning, get in the mirror, fill in the blanks with 3 statements and do this:

1. Look at yourself. For the first time, see you, and remember, your human form is just a human expression of your divine self. You are not your body; fat, short, tall, fit, trim, whatever, that is not you anyway. You can get over it now.
2. Smile. From your eyes, smile.
3. Say out loud, "I'm so proud of you for _____." Fill in the blank with 3 simple statements. You can be proud that you are actually doing this exercise. Whatever you can muster up, congratulate yourself on a job done well.
4. Say, "I love you because _____." Remember, 3 statements.
5. Say, "I forgive you for _____."
6. Say, "Today, I commit to you to _____."

You can expect a host of emotion to come up from doing this. Frustration. Anger. Aggravation. Hurt. Sorrow. Sadness. Pleasure. I can tell you from an experienced person who was not used to loving herself this was very difficult for me and my private clients.

For me, I had a hard time coming up with 3 statements in the beginning. Sometimes it would take several minutes before I could think of anything. But I was determined to fill in the blank three times for each. My self-love teamwork looked like this:

"I am so proud of you because you just keep trying. I am proud of you, Lori, because after all this time, you are still hoping for the best. I am so proud of you, because you still believe there is more for you."

"I love you because you are funny and you crack me up! I love you because you are so creative and your kids believe you can figure anything out. I love you because you are allowing your faith in the process of becoming to sustain you."

"I forgive you for not knowing and thinking you had to know. I forgive you for thinking everyone else knows more than you or are better than you somehow. I forgive you for comparing yourself to anyone else. You did not know your worth."

"Today I commit to you to put down the club and not beat you up when you make a mistake. I commit to you today to pass a mirror and remind you that you are worthy, capable and extraordinary. I commit to you today to not hold anything against you, so that you can have room to grow and learn."

Simple right? Yes, and we both know simple does not equate to easy! But, please do this. It is at least a first step to self-love. I promise you you cannot move forward until you learn to love yourself. There is no way you will fulfill your divine mission in this life without loving you! This really is life or death here. If you want to move forward, self-love is the way.

Self-Acceptance. This might be my most favorite part of FLAG-raising! This is the key to greater creativity: owning your calling and not being timid or shy about who you are. With self-acceptance, you take authority over your divine spiritual gifts, and you use them confidently.

Self-acceptance is self-satisfaction. It's comfort in your own skin. It is happiness from the inside. It is being your own best friend. It is the experience of being so full of yourself that your cup runs over with this goodness. This is what makes you desirable and enviable. A woman who loves herself has accepted who she is and what she came here to do. She is undeniable. She is unstoppable. And she is you.

Self-acceptance is the end of comparisons, because you know there is room for us all. Self-acceptance is the joy of knowing you don't know and you don't care, because everything you need will be drawn to you. It is freedom! There is no competition in self-acceptance, for everyone is a co-laborer.

When you discover who you really are without beliefs, conditioning, rules, or the programs of the world, you are free to accept and love yourself.

Blockages to self-acceptance are validation and approval of others. If you are waiting to be approved of by anyone but yourself, it is a setup for self-rejection every time. But there is something about a woman who is comfortable in her own skin. It's like she smiles from the inside and radiates beauty everywhere.

When you accept who you really are, whatever that looks like for you, you will see others with that same kind of love.

There is nothing to fix. Nobody needs to be saved. You do not have to champion anyone, and you allow others the freedom to be themselves too.

Self-acceptance leads to improved relationships. There will be less resistance in your conversations with people you may not get along with well, but you still love them. You will realize you do not have the change a person and no matter how they see you, you will be ok.

There are some aspects of my path that I do not discuss with the people in my life. It took almost a year to realize that everything does not need explanation or debate. I had to rely on my inner guidance that was still leading me on the path of truth. I've lost some people along the way, but it makes me appreciate who I am even more.

Self-acceptance is magical. It is where you learn your silly, quirky, crazy, thoughtful, loving, imaginative, original TRUE SELF. You learn to accept that sometimes it takes you a little longer to figure stuff out. And it's ok. You accept flaws and imperfections and recognize the perfection in them!

Self-acceptance lets you breathe and live and love without conditions or expectations. This is where you get to be you and everybody else gets to be them.

When you accept who you are, you don't fix anyone, including yourself because there's nothing to fix. You become a breath of fresh air of liberation for everyone around you!

Gratitude. Gratitude is the manifestation of who you really are on the inside, your Higher Self or God-Self showing up in the world as you. Gratitude is where what is in your hand gets multiplied into more than enough.

Gratitude helps you see the simplicity and beauty in everything around you, even what is not so pleasant, because you know it is all working out for your good. Gratitude unlocks blessings and overflow for your life and for others. This is where you see heaven on earth!

Gratitude literally means "readiness to show or express appreciation." This is a state to live in, not just a practice to engage! It is *readiness*. This means you **stay ready** to give and receive gratitude. You ask. You receive. You release. It is a non-stop flow of abundance being heaped on you! Do you want to see more in your life? Be grateful what's already there and even that will be multiplied.

If you have ever known a grateful person, you've seen how easily that person get their needs met. There is no push. There is no strain or struggle. They always have assistance, whether angelic or physical. And life just seems to work for them in all ways.

Gratitude makes you a channel for blessings. A grateful person can be trusted with inner riches, and therefore manifest outer riches with little effort. Gratitude is a multiplier, because as a spiritual force, it is always seeking ways to bring goodness, favor, and abundance your way.

When I was active duty in the Air Force, my last job was a fuels officer. My team and I were responsible for providing fuel and refueling service equipment for military bases all over the world. I learned so much about fuel pipelines and how fuel flows from Texas all the way up the east coast.

I remember learning about the piping and how it is extremely important to keep them clean and free of rust and corrosion. Rusting, dirty pipes contaminates the fuel, damaging vehicles, aircraft, and various types of servicing equipment.

Even though the fuel is what large companies like Exxon, Shell, and the government paid for, if we didn't take extreme care of the pipes the fuel was no good. Putting good fuel in bad pipes contaminated millions of gallons of fuel and wasted billions of dollars.

Your fuel is the spiritual gifts that the world is waiting to enjoy. Your purpose, your calling your heart's desires...all of it is waiting to be served up in a grand way. It's pure and clean. But if your heart is contaminated with comparisons, hurt feelings, resentments, unforgiveness and discontentment you are contaminating the gift.

Your spiritual gifts and talents flow out of your heart. If your heart is the pipes, gratitude is what keeps your pipes clean! Gratitude keeps it all flowing freely from your spirit, through your heart, out to the world.

You don't need more blessings. It would be a misuse of blessing for you to get more and then have it get stuck somewhere in the process of receiving and expressing. Gratitude reminds you that where you are is where you are and it's ok. Where you are is where you're supposed to be to master this level in preparation for the next.

Gratitude is so simple. You are probably already doing it. So now, develop deeper gratitude for what you already have. Increase your gratitude for the natural abundance of life by seeing the blessing in everything around you. Create a greater connection with nature. Observe her and her seasons. She is abundant, lacking nothing, and produces grand things effortlessly and in due timing.

How to play your CARDs

Playing your CARDs is just as simple as raising your FLAG. They go hand-in-hand and happen simultaneously. You don't need to choose which method to use. They are both strong processes that work very well together.

Clear the decks. This refers to heart space. Clearing means keeping yourself aligned in Oneness with Spirit. You never lose your connection, however you can disregard it when your thoughts and intentions take you out of the flow of grace. Clearing happens when You meditate, journal, and spiritual practices that keep You in the vibration of complete Oneness.

ASK. How can you receive if you do not ask? This should be obvious, but think of all the things you struggle with right now. Anything from cleaning your house to starting a business. Most of your problems would be solved with solutions that are already right around you...**if you just ask!** Asking is a faith move. It is an act of trust that demonstrates you know that you are well taken care of and all your needs are met by a simple request for help. Asking requires a level of vulnerability that takes ego all the way out of the equation. It is a direct reflection of your own self-worth because you learn to ask with the expectation that you will get what you've asked for and what you deserve. Make asking a daily and moment by moment practice.

RECEIVE. Now do not hold up the answers by rejecting them! They will come exactly how and when they are supposed to. You stay in receive mode when you are clearing. Stay open and anytime you are given an opportunity to receive something TAKE IT. A compliment. A piece of candy. An offer of lunch. Keep a smile on your face to train your body that you are always in receive mode. A smile shows confidence. It is like saying, "I don't know how or what, but I know what I need is right here for me."

The reason you believe some of your prayers are not being answered, is because you are not receiving. Usually this is because your answer is showing up in a way that you do not expect, and so when it does not *look like* your answer, you reject it. It is the work of your ego mind that will create the story for you that your prayers are never answered. They are! Just stay open to receive the answers however they come to you.

DO. This is action. Notice everything up until this point has been preparing the way for doing...doing does not come first. Because at this point, **all you need is inspiration to direct the doing.** Our society and culture is not set up to encourage you to do this pre-paving. Everything is fast-moving, quick action, get it done now energy. But you can direct your flow to suit YOU. When you use this CARD method, you are in control of your own energy and you're easily directed from within, not by everyone else's priorities.

If you are doing things without clearing, asking and receiving, you are out of order. Stay in order with *inspired* doing. You will get more done, the right things done, with less stress and strain.

These are the tools of coming out of the spiritual closet. These are the keys to living an inspired life in The Yes Process. I have given you the exact things I use in *The Bridge* programs, helping to lay the foundation for you for a powerful ascension into this new way of being yourself.

Raise your FLAG. Play your CARDs. If you stay in this vibration, this could be all you need to accelerate your progress. Just remember, do not seek "the stuff". Seek the kingdom of heaven within you and everything will be added to you.

You can do this. The acronyms are designed to assist your memory, but your spirit already knows this. So please don't try to memorize any of it! Flow with these methods; the simplicity of FLAG allows you to intentionally do things that you're probably already doing. The ease of CARD helps keep you aligned to something that you will never need to "work" at keeping. It just is.

You are powerful beyond what you consciously know. Coming out of your own closet doesn't need to be difficult. Follow these methods and I promise you everything you need for this journey will be attracted to you with the least amount of effort.

Alicia's Story
Stamford, Connecticut

*" My life will never be the same and for that I
am forever grateful to Lori Bell and The Yes
Process.*

*"I came to this program at a low point in my
life. I felt stuck, lost, defeated and just couldn't
seem to find my way. After years of struggling to
do it on my own, I realized that I needed help,
which was difficult for me to admit."*

*"Lori was that Coach/Mentor/Guide that
didn't give me the answers I was looking for. She
led me to the truth of who I am, which holds all
the answers. This was a spirit-led process that
opened me to love, truth and healing. I am now
equipped with the tools to continue saying Yes to
the process of Becoming."*

*"Thank you Lori for providing a loving space
for me to feel safe in taking my mask off."*

*With Love & Gratitude
Alicia*

Phase Three
Dream Life Ascension

Step into the place where dreams are reality, work is play, and abundance is a way of life.

CHAPTER SIX
Portrait Of A Woman
Becoming Herself

My daughter and I watched *The Wiz* with Diana Ross and Michael Jackson about a month ago. I am always fascinated with that story, although I confess I've only recently understood it. Diana Ross ends her time in Oz with a beautiful sentiment she gave the Wizard. The Wiz wanted what Dorothy had. Freedom, friends, courage, plus she was on her way home. He asked her to take him with her. Dorothy replied:

"If you want to get home, I don't know what's in you. You'll have to find that out for yourself. But I do know one thing. You'll never find it in the safety of this room. I tried that all my life and it doesn't work. There's a whole world out there! And you'll have to begin by letting people see who you really are."

My Friend, you are, right now, just like Dorothy. You are not lost. You just have not known where to look for your path back home! If only you had known all you had to do was look inside yourself to discover who you are, where you belong and what you came to do.

The gift has always been there. Your God-Self has been laying dormant your whole life, and when that power is awakened there will be a collision of identity and purpose that will explode within you. You will not contain it or muzzle it. You will overflow with the light and goodness of your own Self as your divine alignment will vibrate in waves from within You and all around You.

I was sleepwalking most of my life. Going along with the crowd and the conditioning of the culture. When I broke the spell, it really was like being born from above. For the first time I understood what being born again really meant.

So many years I spent searching, making it up as I went along, wondering with was wrong with me, when all I had to do was look inside.

What have I learned the most? This is a journey that you must experience. It cannot be taught or read. You must say a full and complete YES if you want to be liberated from thoughts and feelings of inadequacy or deficiency.

I remember when I learned the voice of God within me. It was fascinating to me that the inner voice, which sounded just like mine only wiser, was guiding my thoughts and directing my life. I always thought God was a Being "out there" somewhere, but what I learned through personal experience was any God outside of myself is a created idol. I had the real deal living in me, as Me, and all I had to do was nurture that ongoing dialogue moment by moment.

One day in January 2012, I was journaling. I had just been on social media and after a round of comparing my chapter one to someone else volume two, I was feeling pretty inadequate. So, feeling a tad bit pitiful about myself, I went to my computer.

I keep my journaling in files electronically, a practice I teach as part of TYPUniversity's Divine Blueprint Masterclass. I opened a file and got ready. I remember feeling so heavy inside and I just wanted to hear truth. Actually what I wanted was to hear how successful I am, how wealthy I am, and how much I am in high demand for my brilliance.

So I asked Spirit, "I want to dream with you. Please tell me what is the dream you have for my life here on this earth."

This was a big question, but back then I did not know the magnitude. The dream life that was revealed to me has become the compass for living in abundance. Whenever I'm feeling anything other than prosperous, I know I am not on the path. Using the tools and methods presented here, I can quickly get back into alignment.

The following is a dictation. I remember the feeling of receiving this message, it was as if I knew it without knowing it. I was the Vessel this came through, and it was like one word written was the key to the next word. I didn't judge what I was typing; I only knew that I was typing.

I relaxed and allowed the words to flow from within me, and I'm telling you, it was like a faucet that I could not shut off until the flow was done. This happens to me many times in journaling and when it does, I know what I'm bringing forth is not just my message, but it is for you too.

I originally received this download on January 19, 2012. Since then, it has been refined and reshaped to encapsulate all that is The Yes Process. It highlights rest as a spiritual practice, and knowing your spiritual identity as a way of life.

This is the portrait of a woman who is becoming herself, living her Divine Dream Life:

You are abundantly filled and fulfilled. You awaken and greet Your day with joy and excitement and anticipation of what is happening and what is yet manifesting. You are not stressed because You've reminded yourself that your Divine Team of angels, wisdom of the spirit, and divine resources are with You. You walk heart to heart with the I Am in Your day. You listen for your inner voice, you ask about EVERYTHING and you fellowship. You learn how to nurture and cultivate a deep relationship with Your Spirit.

You have the shortcomings of old programming, but You love Yourself through them and You love the woman You are becoming. You love, forgive and accept Yourself. All is well with You. You attack your responsibilities with fervor and pleasure. No matter what happens to You, You know You can handle anything. Where You are, is where You are supposed to be. You are content with your moments. You are not anxious for anything.

You know "I Am" is taking care of Your dreams and hopes, for they were planted there before You came here. The inner visions and desires that stir Your soul and move Your heart are for You to bring forth in the world and experience them. You are content to just be, for where You are is where You're supposed to be.

You know the "I Am" is opening doors and guiding You to walk right on through them. You and God are One. You allow the fullest expression of your God-Self to flow through You in everything You do because You have discovered Your real true divine identity. Anything You ask for in faith and imagination is an automatic done deal. You want for nothing. You are complete and whole in who You really are and You love it. You are living a satisfied, complete, abundant life!

Admittedly, when I originally received this, it was a little weird. I didn't get it.

I said, "Um, God, this is not a dream life! This is boring! I wanted to hear you say something like how you see me on international stages and making millions doing what I love."

I laugh at this now. Because the response was this:

"I know. You want the stuff. That's your dream. But once you lay down that dream for the substance within You, You will attract the stuff. If you stop seeking the stuff and pursue the kingdom, You'll get the stuff."

I get it now. All my life I had been seeking stuff. Success. Fame. Notoriety. Anything to make me happy. Now I know, and now I get to show you the way too.

A woman who has become herself gathers her strength from the well that never runs dry within her. She knows the value of stillness, breaking away from the noise so she can hear the inner guidance that beckons to her from within.

She knows that every situation and circumstance confronting her is met by her divine identity, and so there is *no thing* she cannot overcome.

A Becoming Woman is confident in her ability to generate her power from within. There is ease and grace in how she leads her life. Oh, life still happens. Tragedy still comes to her door. Disappointment still threatens to steal her joy. But her secret is in the way she believes, loves and lights her own way.

She understands her standing as a spiritual being. Where others are confused about where God is, a Becoming Woman knows her God, for the spirit of God is *her*. Living, being and expressing itself as Love personified through the Woman.

The Becoming Woman does not ask how, she is only concerned with "who". She declares her identity and is a Woman of Great Faith. She boldly thrives in her gifts of seeing, hearing and speaking in the Spirit.

She is a warrior who brings the full strength of who she is to the fight and is never overcome by life. There is no such thing as defeat for the Becoming Woman. Because even losing is winning for a woman living from the inside out.

Everything and everybody associated with her is connected to blessing, favor, and a release of her God-Presence. The Becoming Woman is highly esteemed and highly favored. She walks the path of the courageous, daring to search out the inner riches of her heart to reveal her true identity.

She walks through the dirty ugly of her life and past experiences. She knows the pain of rejection, and she has felt the shame and guilt of not rising up into her calling. She is humble and gives freely of herself, while stewarding her energy and establishing boundaries.

She is served because she serves humanity in her bold calling and purpose. She chooses heart-work over hard work and reaps massive rewards in half the time.

Functioning as a Vessel, the Becoming Woman discovers the mysteries that have been hidden for her since the beginning. Because she is faithful to her inner work, she is given the blueprints, master keys, divine ideas and strategies for which most work hard. Material wealth manifests with ease. Opportunities that she does not ask for nor plans for seem to fall into her lap.

Most of all, the Becoming Woman leads her life from the most secure, peaceful, joyous place. Peace that passes understanding overtakes her. Joy unspeakable is a daily affair. She leads her life from the inside out.

She is tried, tested and proven. Her journey is

not perfect. But she dies daily to arise more confident, stronger, wiser and loving than the day before.

This woman I am describing is not a fantasy made up person. THIS IS WHO YOU ARE.

You *are* enough.

You *are* worthy.

You *are* deserving.

You *are* chosen.

You *are* the One.

You are the only One you have been waiting for.

Go into this next season of your life with the assurance that you are not working your way into something miraculous...you are *already* living the miraculous! You are not on a search to find...*you are on a journey of discovery*! You've already found.

Using what I have presented here in this how-to guide, perfect your understanding of what you have. Make room. Make way for discovery. Make time to abide, dwell, discover, imagine, read, hear and do. What you are seeking you ALREADY ARE. YOU ALREADY HAVE.

Love, blessing, peace and light to you!

Christina's Story
St. Louis, Missouri

"Prior to discovering The Yes Process on Facebook and working with Lori in The Bridge, my biggest fear was not reaching my full potential. I knew I am here for a big life mission, but I thought it was the things I DIDN'T have that kept me stuck."

"When I enrolled in The Bridge, I was ready. I was ready to attack my financial issues, my lifestyle situation, and my goals and dreams with a vengeance! I was doing the exact opposite of what Lori teaches. I was working from the outside in. I had said Yes with my enrollment, but not Yes to The Cave. I wasn't yet 'all in'."

"Lori's coaching style was just what I needed to say Yes to loving and honoring myself. She really was the guide pointing the way, and all I needed to do was open up and face what I had been avoiding all my life: feelings of unworthiness."

"If you're looking for someone who gets where you are, is faithful to her own work, and delivers a systematic program that empowers you to move your life forward, Lori and The Bridge are the answer to your prayer."

CHAPTER SEVEN
Final Thoughts and Next Steps

So what now? What do you do with all this? How can you incorporate the work of The Yes Process in your life?

If you have been inspired by the material presented here, I am glad. But it is not for your inspiration. It is for your *integration*. If you have been feeling stuck, unmotivated to finish what you start, or feel overwhelmed but the thoughts that threaten you will never release your potential, this book was written for you. You are holding in your hands the blueprint I have used for my own life and with the clients and students I support.

In Part 1, I showed you how to clear the mental clutter by shifting your focus from doing the hard outer work to inner work where your real power is. I gave the secret to shutting out the noise with a 7-day Lifestyle Observation, so you can allow space in your life for your real true message to emerge.

I shared how to fill the space of doing with being, and helped you understand the flow of divine energy from your Higher Source. When you know your divine connection you also know you can never disconnect. You can undermine and disregard, but your divine connection is sure. Following the guidance in this section will help you keep your awareness raised to who you really are.

Then in Part 2, we entered "The Cave" of your heart where the real treasure is buried. This is the deep dark parts where we would rather cover up by eating it away, sexing it away, shopping it away, or doing anything we can in order to NOT deal with ourselves. This is where true courage allows you to see the truth you have been seeking.

I showed you how to come out of the spiritual closet. Being bold with your beliefs and shedding those fear-based beliefs that no longer resonate with the person you are becoming. In order to come out to the world, you must come out to yourself first. It can be scary, but with the tools presented here, you are well equipped.

You learned the powerful and simple techniques of raising your FLAG and playing your CARDs. You have permission now, to have fun with this journey you are on! It is ok to mess up, get it right, fall down and get back up. You are having a human experience and practicing these divinely inspired tools just helps your flow through with grace and ease.

Finally in Part 3, you entered Divine Recovery. I presented a clear picture of a woman who is becoming herself. It is not a measuring stick. It is a horizon that you are walking into day-by-day, moment-by-moment. You will know you are here by the releasing of tension in your body, emotions that you use as a gauge of where you are aligned, and activities that you either adopt or just leave behind. It is a powerful place from which to live. And you are becoming her every time you say yes.

You have it in you to be and become all that you came here for. I encourage you to use this book as a guide and read it several times, maybe even once monthly. I wrote this as an easy, non-threatening read that you can accomplish in one sitting.

If you read this through once, great! Now go back and read it a chapter at a time. Make notes in the margins or use a journal so you can ask your own questions to see where are you in all this.

While you are reading, you can add more depth to your experience when you visit www.theyesprocessbook.com. There are videos I have loaded just for readers of this book that compliment the chapters. You'll see my personal stories, and read and hear stories of others who have overcome their spiritual and personal struggles by using The Yes Process book.

Any journey you take is way more fun when you do it with friends! My personal mission is to help usher in a new era where living your dreams is the new normal. I equip individuals and groups with the spiritual and practical tools to help them operate boldly in their destinies. This is The Yes Process. It is the blueprint for how to create a life of purpose, passion, and impact.

I want you to share this mission with your girlfriend circles, organizations, or book clubs. I believe that each of us are responsible for the expression of our gifts and the energy we are putting out into the world. This book is just my expression. The vibrations that are present here are meant to spread love throughout the world. So when you share this, you're a part of the change we all want to see in the world. A more loving human-kindness.

How You Can Get More

I am so grateful for The Yes Process! I truly see this work as separate from myself. I am the Vessel and channel through which it is delivered. In The Yes Process, I created a proprietary system that I used as my own personal process. I STILL use these principles.

What makes The Yes Process so unique is that I have walked through every single method, solution or technique that I teach. When I was in the beginning stages of discovering this journey I knew there was something I was missing. I just didn't know what.

But I did know one thing: I could not become who I needed to be by myself. There was too much gap between where I was and what I wanted to be. So I reached out and got the support of a strong mentor who had walked through her cave too, and on the other side were her lessons and experiences that pointed me, not to her way, *but to my Source within me.*

What I needed for myself was a bridge over to the other side. With her help, I found myself. I found my voice, my truth and energized my spiritual gifts. I learned that it's ok to change my beliefs even when they go against culture and upbringing. I learned how to bridge the gap of confusion with clarity, and filled in the spaces of clutter with guidance.

That is why I created **The Bridge Transformation**

program. Remember, if you knew how to do this, you would have done it by now! That is the position I was in, and I was done being frustrated by it. So I committed to the path of YES and did my work. Now I get to help you do yours.

The Bridge Transformation is designed for the woman who:

• Is accustomed to working hard to reach goals, striving to reach the next level of success, but still not reaping the rewards of the work.

• Is searching, seeking and questioning. She knows there is something missing from her life, that she's right on the edge of a breakthrough, but just can't seem to break free.

• Feels emotionally blocked or stuck and lacks clarity of where to start and what to do next.

• Isn't sure how to trust her inner guidance to help her move forward.

• Is overwhelmed by daily tasks and responsibilities and struggles to balance the daily demands of life with doing what she's really called to do.

• Is unsure of her true purpose.

• Is riddled with self-doubt, low self-confidence and fearful of making any forward progress.

Find out more about The Bridge Transformation Program at www.theyesprocessbook.com.

Enroll in TYPUniversity! It is the online training school designed to help you discover and establish your divine purpose and identity. The core curriculum is based on The Yes Process principles of clearing blockages to receiving guidance and expressing your gifts. TYPU is self-paced and packed full of classes that you take online as quickly or slowly as you like. If you like building your own support community of like-minded women who are moving in the same direction, you will enjoy TYPUniversity.

Masterclasses are added routinely, and they are all based

on what you have read and learned here. This book is a great starting point. Masterclasses are a great way to steadily add to your knowledge base and spiritual toolkit. Find out more about The Yes Process University at www.theyesprocessbook.com.

Bring The Yes Process to your organization! Now available for virtual gatherings like webinars or tele-classes, or live speaking engagements, you can help your audience move through the challenges of functioning in their identity with feminine power and grace. Email support@theyesprocess.com to discuss how The Yes Process can support your next event.

Ways To Spread The Word and Support Others

I have not shared this out loud yet, but here goes. I have a personal mission to get *The Yes Process* into the hands of 100,000 people in one year. I truly believe when people really learn and live their true identity, not only will they change their own life, but they have the power to transform neighborhoods, organizations, nations and the planet! Love is the revolutionary solution to the hurt in the human soul. But it starts with YOU. One person at a time.

Culture always presents an opportunity to lament on the ills of the world. If you take a worldly perspective, you will agree that there is so much wrong here. But it doesn't have to be that way. There is so much right here too, two very powerful, very influential elements you may have over looked: **You and Me.**

How do you change the world? How do you end poverty, and war, and trafficking, and planetary devastation? The answer is simple. It starts with the two elements.

If I elevate myself to the point of forgiving myself for what I did not know or understand, how much forgiveness would I have for you cutting me off in traffic?

If I were patient and loving with myself as I parented my children and allowed space for their mistakes, what could that mean for their experiences with your kids on the playground?

If I were to accept who I am in this human experience, as wacky and weird as I can be, would I really care how you looked, dressed or what your sexuality is?

And if I were grateful, and I mean filled to overflowing with gratitude about where I am, who I am and whatever is going on with me, wouldn't that include being grateful for you too?

So you see, in what seems like a small way, if you learned to master the techniques here, you can literally transform the world. But it starts with what you do now. What you believe about you. How you act.

With this in mind, here are a few ideas you can use to be part of this greater mission:

• Buy an extra copy of *The Yes Process* for a friend. This can be a great secret surprise, birthday gift, or a just-because way to love on someone special.

• If you have a platform, a stage, a following or a soapbox, tweet or post about The Yes Process to your own people! Use hashtag #typbook or #theyesprocess in your posts.

• Are you an event host? Buy copies of the book in bulk and resell to your organizations at your events! You keep all the profits to raise money for your cause AND you help spread the message of The Yes Process.

• Are you a traveling speaker or author? Need product to fill your table? You can buy this book in bulk and provide your audience with even more variety and resources to build their success library. Again, keep whatever profit you make from the sale.

• Host an online discussion about a topic from the book! Send a message to support@theyesprocess.com with an invitation so I can attend the party!

• Follow The Yes Process on Facebook and share quotes from the book and inspirational photos with your audience.

• Post your motivating review on Amazon for other readers! You are very influential, you know.

You can find The Yes Process:

About the Book: www.theyesprocessbook.com
Website/Blog: www.theyesprocess.com
Facebook: www.fb.com/TheYesProcess
Pinterest: www.pinterest.com/TheYesProcess
IG: www.instagram.com/TheYesProcess
Media Inquiries: support@theyesprocess.com

ACKNOWLEDGEMENTS

I thank God. I have been led in extraordinary ways to deliver this message. Let this work be a symbol of my continued commitment to my calling, to be the Vessel and Herald I came here to be. I am so grateful for the day I learned to hear God from inside me, for when I learned God lived through me, as me. I am thankful for the journey that brought me here.

My husband, Kenyon. You have experienced my dark and bathed in my light, and you have loved them both. Thank you for allowing me the freedom to explore who I am and giving me a safe place to sort it all out. It has been a crazy ride, but I am grateful we are on it together.

Our children Amira, Kenyon II, Roman and fur baby Thunder. In your own way, each of you have pulled just a little more "Me" out of myself. You have challenged me in just about every way possible! Just when I thought I was done, we added Thunder. All of you together are my greatest teachers in this life. I love you.

My parents, Charles and Patricia Riley. My daddy was everything to our family and his transition in 2008 devastated us all. But I am so thankful for all that he taught me and how he prepared me for life. To my mom for being strong in tough times and showing me what it looks like to win. I love you.

My sister, Kia. Everyone should be blessed with a sister like you. Thank you for your support and listening ear even when you did not understand.

My entire extended family for supporting what I do over all these years.

To my business mentor Fabienne Fredrickson and fellow members of Boldheart Academy. Without you guys I would not have had the courage to write this book. I did it first and thought about it second! Thank you for pushing me forward.

My soul sisters of the "new school". Thank you

for helping me see that becoming myself did not need to be a lonely place. In your own way, each of you have pulled me up when I felt like I needed to hide. Thank you for answering the phone, the email, the text, and for giving me a safe place to grow, stretch, and learn: Karin Haysbert of The Queens for Christ, my cousin Jarmila Price, Britt Johnson of You.Are.Venus, Chelsea Bella, Malena Crawford of The Black Divine Feminine Reawakened, Dejarré Heal, and Namaste Moore of the School of Feminine Transformation.

My spiritual and personal mentor, Molesey Crawford of The Queen Code. Your life is a blueprint. I did NOT know what I was getting into with you!! But you helped me excavate the courage I needed to say YES and to keeping saying it, until I can now turn around and tell it to others. I am liberated because of what you taught me.

My clients and students. You trust me with your stories, your heart, your time, your money, your attention and your dreams. You lift me and remind me that above all else, stay committed to the work within. We are both teachers and students. I love you.

ABOUT THE AUTHOR

Lori Bell is a USAF veteran, award-winning military spouse and creator of The Yes Process lifestyle. After leaving the military, Lori did what most people do when trying to reinvent, rediscover or simply find a happy place: *she did stuff.*

Lori started the first-ever online support group for military moms and spouses, and earned awards and accolades for her work in the military spouse community. But at the end of all that was just more "doing", more keeping up, and more proving her self-worth.

Finally, Lori became her own best student. She took a one year hiatus from projects and accomplishments to face what she now calls "The Cave", the place where fear is overcome and truth is discovered.

From her own heart-work in The Cave, facing herself and accepting her calling, The Yes Process was born. Lori now enjoys fulfilling work that feels like play, a growing client base, and a thriving entrepreneurial business.

Lori's military spouse work has been featured in front of more than 30 million people through national media including *Military Spouse Magazine, Oprah Winfrey Network, Lifetime Television Network, NBC Nightly News "Making a Difference", Good Morning America, CNN, Fox News,* and *The Huffington Post.*

Lori enjoys life with her active duty husband Kenyon and their three children wherever the Air Force sends them.